Monday Morning Memoirs

Monday Morning Memoirs

Women in the Second Half of Life

edited by
Maureen Murdock

This book was printed in the United States of America.

To order additional copies of this book, contact:
Xlibris Corporation
1-888-795-4274
www.Xlibris.com
Orders@Xlibris.com
14939

Contents

CHAPTER ONE

Childhood

CHAPTER TWO

Family

CHAPTER THREE

Mothers

CHAPTER FOUR

Fathers

CHAPTER FIVE

Children

CHAPTER SIX

Marriage

CHAPTER SEVEN

Body

CHAPTER EIGHT

Reflections

BIBLIOGRAPHY

CONTRIBUTORS

INTRODUCTION

The women writers in this book were originally strangers who met by chance in a memoir class I taught in the UCLA Extension Writers' Program in the mid-nineties and became strong allies in the intervening years. After the class ended, these nine women, aged forty-five to seventy-nine, decided to continue writing together and asked me to go on working with them. They couldn't imagine losing the opportunity to hear the evolving tale of each other's life.

At first we met weekly in my house in Venice and when I moved to Santa Barbara we continued to meet monthly. On the first Monday of each month, these nine brave souls carpool up the coast to my house in the hills overlooking a field where an aging mare, one donkey, and two frisky fillies play. The octogenarian owner of the field, Mr. Pozzebon, also pushes rocks around from one section of the field to another, we think, for our amusement.

We have met for five years listening to each other's writing through the various life events that occur in the span of half a decade: adolescents leaving home; births of grandchildren, deaths of parents, chronic illnesses of friends; accomplishments of children, the woes of expanding waistlines; the pain of facelifts, separation, and divorce; house buying alone; retirement; and furtive love affairs in hotels. Throughout this process of reconstructing our lives, we have chosen the words to describe our longings, fears, pain, doubts, wonder, joy, humor, grief, and hopes for the future.

*   *   *

Women have always gathered to tell their stories—that is nothing new. Whether they were cooking or sewing together, talking about their children while waiting for them at the bus stop or in the carpool line, trading gossip in the ladies room, battle scars in the faculty room, or political strategies in the conference room, women talked. Famous women have revealed the intimate details of their loves and lives in the fields of publishing, entertainment, business, and politics. But what is new for ordinary women, women whose lives have not been lived in the limelight, is to write their memoirs.

In years past, women only revealed their innermost thoughts and feelings to their diary, their spouse, sometimes a close friend or sister if they were lucky; oftentimes, a therapist, if they could afford one. But now women of all ages and cultural backgrounds are coming together to write about their life experiences in memoir form; to hand down their narratives to the women and men who come after them.

This wildly different, yet amazingly similar group of women have developed a uniquely close, yet periodic relationship, unfettered by the responsibilities and obligations of social friendships. Although they read stories about each other's spouses, children, parents, friends and lovers, if they were to come face-to-face with these people they would not know them. Nor would they be known to them, except perhaps by name. So the lack of a shared social life allows a particular freedom to be self-reflective. As Dorothy writes:

"We are non-judgmental women of vastly different ages,
life styles and heritage who, respectful of our differences,

embrace our similarities while learning the difference
between an exchange of the secrets of every day life with
social friends, and giving full voice to our inner selves
when we meet monthly as allies."

Each woman brings a thirst for learning and the seeds of trust to the group and as they hone their writing skills together, the trust has grown strong and deep. The fact that these women are mature enough to accept each other's experiences, wise enough to laugh at themselves, and accomplished enough to forgo the negative criticism, competition, and envy that often seeps into a writing group has helped the trust deepen. Only that underlying assurance of safety could have allowed each woman the freedom to open chapters of her life she may have shared with no one else. Each converted the childhood dare, "I'll Show You Mine if You Show Me Yours" into another more knowing form.

Every woman brought to the group her own unique life experience, the desire to find the right words to describe the experience, the panoply of people involved, and the feelings unearthed from the particular memory as well as her strengths and weaknesses discovered in the writing. Stories buried since childhood, incidents too painful to ponder, too embarrassing to admit, emerged into consciousness in this atmosphere of compassion and support. The fact that we are a multi-generational group only adds to its rich complexity; we all learn from each other. As Hillary wrote:

"The safe and nurturing environment that has been
created by these women allows me to read aloud material
I have wept over my computer writing. When you feel
people will catch you with kind hands, it makes it easier
to run and jump into unknown terrain."

Each woman has gained freedom and boldness in our safe container and each has re-remembered the value of her life.

Although the importance of building trust in a writing group seems self-evident, the degree to which a writing group succeeds depends largely upon the respect each person learns, by example, to extend to others in the group. Respect is the corner stone of interpersonal trust and it must be carefully reinforced for vulnerable memories to come to the surface and find voice. Over time, each writer in our group began to feel safe enough to reveal her life experiences and confident enough in her own writing to make constructive suggestions for the improvement of others' writing. The enthusiasm in this group for each writer's attempts and successes support the overall writing process of all. Critiques are based on whether a piece successfully includes the elements of memoir as well as tension and insight and I make suggestions about the mechanics of writing and sentence structure.

It is a well-documented fact that the best writers are readers so each time we meet we read aloud and discuss excerpts from well-written published memoirs to examine how they succeed (or do not succeed) as memoirs. Writers such as Mary Karr, Nuala O'Faolain, Geoff Wolff, Vivian Gornick, Alice Kaplan, May Sarton, Flor Fernandez Barrios, Alice Walker, bell hooks, Rick Bragg, James McBride, Mary McCarthy, Frank McCourt, Dave Eggers, Kim Chernin, Pierre DeLattre and scores of others serve not only as models but as stimulation for self reflection—a quality essential to memoir writing.

Each time we meet, I suggest a topic for the next session but these are suggestions only and any topic of the writer's choosing is acceptable. The aim of the memoir group is to nurture the creativity of each woman, not to set boundaries on what material is appropriate. It is almost inevitable that each woman in the group would, at some time, write about her mother, father, siblings, spouse, children or friends with whom she has had close relationships because these actors are inseparable from our memories of ourselves. Hence this book is divided not only into stages of life development but also addresses these important relationships in our lives.

What is a Memoir?

A memoir is how a writer remembers the events of her life, chronicling the journey, as memoirist Mary Karr has written, from there to here. But rather than simply recounting an incident or a memory from her life, the memoirist both tells the story and muses upon it, trying to unravel what it means in the light of her current knowledge.

Memories reflect the dreams, desires, and emotions we all share. The memoir presupposes that there is a certain unity to human experience; that we all share similar hopes and emotions. When a writer is telling us a story about herself, she is talking about all of us to some degree. The essence of memoir is to participate in the writer's struggle to achieve some understanding of the events, traumas, and triumphs of her personal recollection. For a memoir to be a memoir it must include *self-reflection*.

In *The Daughter of the Queen of Sheba*, her memoir of growing up with a mother who was manic depressive, National Public Radio correspondent Jackie Lyden writes of the task of the memoirist reflecting upon her life, "We have survived, we are at the end of our journey, we want to, like Odysseus, make some sense of where we have gone . . . That means we must have digested the experience, not merely confessed it. We must have a little compassion for the selves that we are delving into here, not a sense of revenge or self-pity. The only truth that is universal for memoirs is the truth applicable to any good piece of writing: it must transform our experience of what it is to be human."

When we tell our story and tell it well, in a way that it reflects the *universal* experience of being human, we become a part of each other. Henry Miller was fond of saying: "The mission of man on earth is to remember." To re-member. To put back together. When I write about my mother who is dead, I am putting her back together and passing her on to the reader in the only way I can—passing her on as memory. When I write about her and our relationship I try to bring her alive in the most honest way I can for a moment. This moment. I learn something about myself and her and the nature of mothers and daughters every time I do.

Memoir is not an autobiography relaying events from birth to death but rather a *selected aspect of a life*. How the writer selects that aspect is crucial to the success of her piece. The writer has to know—not necessarily right away, but at some point—what it is she really wants to write about, which in turn will tell her what to leave out. Being willing to leave things out is vital.

The essence of a memoir is the track of a person's thoughts struggling to make sense out of an event. The memoir tries to frame an experience that could have been little more than chaotic at the time, with amazing moments of insight and struggle. This is the healing power of memoir; the reader enters into the author's desire to make meaning from the fragments of her life and begins to draw the puzzle pieces of her own life together as well.

A memoir is written in *a casual, conversational style*; no long—winded sentences are needed but plenty of *wit* is welcome. It is as if the writer sits down with a close friend over a cup of tea to tell an *intimate story*; this is what happened and what I now understand about it. She tells us her personal experiences, opinions and prejudices.

The memoirist must be a *reliable narrator*; if she stays at the same flat level of self-disclosure and understanding throughout, we will not believe her; particularly if she portrays herself as a perennial victim or a goody-two-shoes. The struggle for *honesty* is central to the memoir. The trick for the memoirist is to be able to laugh at herself and to realize that she herself is not important except to illuminate a human trait so that others will feel less alone and odd. So the elements of memoir writing that we strive to include are remembered event, universal theme, casual conversational style, reliability as a narrator, intimacy, honesty, humor and insight. When you read the memoirs in this book, look for the elements of memoir they feature.

What is wonderful about this collection of memoirs you are about to read is that each writer demonstrates the ability to have compassion for and humor about herself even in the midst of some of life's great challenges. This gift of perspective and wisdom is one that we give each other and now give to you. We welcome you into our lives and hope that you will recognize a bit of yourself there too.

Maureen Murdock

CHAPTER ONE

Childhood

What is it about memoir that touches us so deeply? Memoirs explore the past to understand the present and memoirs of childhood illustrate the fact that seeds planted in our youth have enormous impact on who we become as adults. When we read about a writer's childhood we too remember the innocence we felt when life was not as compartmentalized as it is now and "getting out of school for the summer" really meant time to daydream, explore, observe nature, have adventures, eat hotdogs and watermelon, and hang out with friends. A friendlier time. A more spacious time. A time to reflect, observe others, feel the grass under our bare feet, fall in love.

In discussing why she wrote *An American Childhood*, Annie Dillard once said, "A child wakes up over and over again, and notices that she's living. A child dreams along, loving the exuberant life of the senses, in love with beauty and power, oblivious of herself, and then suddenly, bingo, she wakes up and feels herself alive."

Because time is more spacious in childhood or perhaps because a child is closer to the ground and the world is a brand new frontier, many memoirs of childhood are rich in sensual details; the writer's memory of smells, tastes, colors, textures and sounds is vivid. Whenever I give students the assignment to write a first childhood memory or their first lunchtime at school, the written details amaze me. How can anyone in their forties, fifties, or sixties remember the exact sensation associated with their first taste of brown sugar sandwiches when they were six or the smell of peanut butter and jelly sandwiches when they were five? The answer is that those initial sense experiences remain distinct. What we see, taste, smell and observe in childhood sticks. In writing about the house she loved as a child, memoirist Alice Kaplan writes: "I loved to hide in that house. I hid under the grand piano, to watch the argyle socks of my sister's dates. I crouched on the staircase, to watch my parents' parties. I hid behind the couch. Everyone had an activity I wanted to observe."

Memoirs of adolescence are filled more with emotional than sensual details: the intense feelings of longing, belonging, or wanting to belong and the physical changes that accompany puberty. Almost every woman, no matter how old she is, remembers the first time she got her period or fell in love and those memories carry an unforgettable feeling tone.

In *French Lessons*, Alice Kaplan writes of adolescence: "I didn't know what age I was. Chronologically I was twelve, but I corresponded more closely to the Gesell chapter on age sixteen. I thought I might be even older inside and was forced to live as a child . . . . I thought that getting my period early was a test, to see if I could take care of myself. My body had gone on ahead of me to see if I could catch up." Her description of her body having a mind of its own captures the universality of adolescent physical confusion experienced by both genders.

As you read the memoirs in this section, notice whether the writer includes the elements of memoir discussed in the Introduction. Is there a remembered event that has universal appeal—something that you can relate to from your own early life or the life of a friend or family member? Do you find the narrator's voice authentic? Do you believe her? Is her style casual and conversational enough to invite you into the intimacy of her experience? Does she have enough distance from the event and enough maturity at present to reflect on its meaning? Does some experience in her life resonate with your own? These childhood memoirs remind us about a child's self-discovery, her growing recognition of her own presence in the world, and her early awareness of the conditions of others around her.

In "Brown Sugar Sandwiches," Brooke Anderson writes about her memory at six of meeting her grandmother for the first time. The careful preparations her mother takes to dress her and comb her hair prepares the reader for a rather elegant encounter. The details Anderson uses to describe her grandmother's entrance and "English style tea" informs the reader that this grandmother of the full length tomato colored chiffon gown and leopard turban is no ordinary everyday grannie spreading butter and spooning brown sugar on a piece of bread.

"She placed the brown sugar sandwich on a flowered china dessert plate and cut it diagonally in half," Anderson writes. "'Here my little one.' I took a bite. It was a strange sensation. The molasses hiding in the brown sugar was harsh and sweet at the same time. An extravagant taste."

Anderson invites the reader into this intimate scene with her exquisite details and the reader is carried back to a universal moment in childhood when child and grandparent share a hidden secret or forbidden delicacy absent the hovering parent. The remembered event, that first bite of her grandmother's brown sugar sandwich, becomes a metaphor for the innocent pleasure of childhood when a young girl or boy can still taste the simple sweetness of life and savor dreams of a bounteous future.

Jacqueline Connolly's "The Cost of Asking" reminds us that adolescence is a time of risk taking and opportunities that only come once. Jackie describes her shock and delight in seeing her movie idol, Robert Mitchum, in the same non-Commissioned Officer's Club where her stepfather is stationed and having the gumption to ask for his autograph. She describes perfectly the mixed pleasure and embarrassment she experiences as a sixteen-year-old as she contemplates approaching him. "I couldn't help blushing. Not just a rosy glimmer, but a deep scarlet eruption." Crushes for Connolly were never casual and her blushing did not bolster her confidence.

Reflecting on this event fifty something years later, Jackie realized how much courage it took for her to approach Mitchum. Their interchange became a watermark in her development. He teased her at first, flattered to be asked by an attractive ingenue and then wrote her a personal note. Jackie wrote "The Cost of Asking" in response to an assignment I had given to write about an adolescent rite of passage. A phone call from her daughter announcing Mitchum's death jogged Jackie's memory about the importance of the event. It wasn't until after she wrote the piece and read it to the group that she realized how much a rite of passage this encounter had been for her.

Dorothy Huebel hails from South Dakota and her memoir of childhood recalls a particular time in U.S. prairie life when "hobos" still hopped freight trains in all kinds of weather and went from town to town working for their food and a place to sleep. One of the elements of memoir writing is context: placing a remembered event within a social or historical framework. Dorothy does just that with "Prairie Sage." She describes a slice of life that has all but disappeared from modern life even though hunger and homelessness remain a constant. In addition, she reflects about how the most unlikely friendships begun in childhood become some of the most valuable beacons of wisdom in later life.

Dorothy's writing also demonstrates a universal trait of young children who closely observe and listen to those around them. She assumes she knows how her mother will feel and react to the arrival of this hobo:

> "Knowing my mother, I know how distressed she must have been at the thought of sending this man out doors without the clothing he needed to withstand the bitter weather. And I'm sure she asked herself where he and the hundreds of others like him, who during the depression crossed the country looking for work, slept while storms raged and temperatures dropped. I stayed in the kitchen while he ate and she went down to the basement."

As you will read, Dorothy also captures the colloquialisms and cadence of the prairie sage's speech. In memoir writing, it is particularly important to express the unique vocabulary and sentence structure which is so revelatory of a character's nature. Even if you can not remember the exact dialogue, try to get a feel for how you think the person would say something. If you start to pay close attention to what is said by those around you now, chances are you will develop a good ear for remembered dialogue. Finally, the compassion displayed by the young Dorothy for the wandering Clyde foreshadows the woman who came to run a large social service agency in California.

THE COST OF ASKING

By Jacqueline Connolly

When my daughter, Angela, called mid-afternoon from Washington and said, "Oh, Mom. I just heard the news—I'm so sorry!", I immediately went into my panic state—what now after all the other set-backs of this last year?

"Why, what's happened?" I asked.

"Robert Mitchum, of course. Didn't you hear? He died this morning. Another loss you have to deal with."

I had to smile to think that she was putting a movie actor, the romantic idol of my youth, in the same category as the recent death of two close friends.

"Oh, Honey. That's very sweet of you but I knew he was getting old so his death isn't really a surprise."

"Well, Mom," she said, "I'm glad you're not letting it upset you because I know how crazy you were about him."

After she hung up, I realized with a little tinge, that actually I did feel sad about his death: one more door softly closed. One more hero down. How long had it been since that historic day?

I was fifteen at the time; my stepfather was stationed at Fort MacArthur, a military installation in close proximity to Hollywood. During the summer I would spend my days swimming and lounging around the Post's large pool until late in the afternoon when hunger would drive me and my friends over to the Non-Commissioned Officers' Club where they served juicy cheeseburgers and thick chocolate malts. On this particular day, I was with my girlfriend, Rae, and another Army offspring, Austin Ingram. Austin and I were "casually" interested in each other.

The NCO club consisted mainly of a huge warehouse-like room with a bar stretching across one end where everyone would put in their order and then wait nearby until it was ready. It was always crowded with soldiers, and those few civilians allowed in usually sat in a group of tables set along the perimeter of the room, separate from the military. This afternoon, as we waited for our order, I froze. I couldn't believe what I was hearing behind me. Could it possibly be the deep, slow, hypnotic voice that I dreamed of every night? I kept listening, thinking I must be crazy but no, it was him. Only the sultry throat of the man whose slow sleepy eyes on the movie screen sent bolts of lightning surging through my body could utter those husky notes: my idol, Robert Mitchum! Breathing deeply, I mustered the courage to turn around and there he stood, wearing Army fatigues and casually conversing with some other soldiers.

What to do? Although he had been in only a few movies, I knew the first time I saw him and heard him speak in a "B" western, "West of the Pecos," that I was hooked. I scanned through all the movie magazines—there were no posters then—to see if any carried his picture. When I found ones that did, I would buy them, carefully cut the photos out and tape them to the wall of my bedroom. No one else could claim that space—only Robert Mitchum.

When my order was ready, I carried it to the table where my friends were seated and stammered out my discovery. We watched as Robert and his buddies walked to a table situated right in the center of all the other soldiers.

I *had* to have his autograph, but how? Knowing that boys

were supposed to be braver, I turned to Austin with a cajoling smile and asked: "Will you get his autograph for me?"

He looked at the intimidating crowd stationed between our tables and laughed: "I don't want his autograph; if you want it, you get it!" Timid Rae, I knew, was hopeless.

I didn't know what to do. It was not only shyness that held me back, it was also the fact that whenever I drew attention, however slight, I couldn't help blushing. Not just a rosy glimmer, but a deep scarlet eruption! This was the scourge of my life, a dead giveaway of how insecure I was feeling no matter how poised I might try to appear. Since this curse generated lots of teasing, I often kept quiet when I wanted to express myself, not willing to risk humiliation.

I sat there and pleaded with myself: "You'll never get this opportunity again—it's definitely now or never!" But how could I brave that terrifying wall of khaki, endless rows of loud men ranting at each other through a haze of cigarette smoke and clinking bottles of beer. I just couldn't. "But if you don't, you know you'll hate yourself for being such a coward; you'll have to live with that shame, that sense of loss, the rest of your life."

I tore off a sheet of paper gathered from some scraps in the trash, felt myself stand up and with my heart pounding so hard I knew everyone could see it vibrate, I started toward his table. Keeping my head down, placing one foot in front of the other while trying desperately not to meet anyone's eyes, I kept saying to myself: "If I don't see them, they won't see me or, at least, I don't have to *know* they see me."

Finally, I reached his table. Startled, he looked up. I placed the scrap of paper down in from of him and muttered: "May I please have your autograph?"

Was it my imagination or was the whole room suddenly silent, everyone staring at me? Already bright red, now I was on fire. I would have ignited anyone who touched me.

He looked up at me and asked, "Why?"

"Because you're Robert Mitchum," I replied, trembling.

He smiled, "No, I'm not."

Oh, God, I prayed, please don't let him tease me! What am I going to do?

And then I heard this squeaky sound sputter out of me: "Yes, you are. I know by your voice."

Dumb, dumb, dumb! As if anyone couldn't tell just by looking at him! Maybe I could faint like I do in Church; that would be dramatic. By now the glow emanating from my body must be heating the whole room. No one could escape witnessing my distress.

Then he smiled and said, "What's your name?"

"Jackie."

He started writing and with a reassuring grin, handed the paper to me. I thanked him and clutching my prize, crept hurriedly back to my table. I knew my friends were embarrassed for me and embarrassed for themselves, too, since they were with this pathetic creature. Actually, I think "disgusted" would describe Austin's expression.

Rae broke the silence: "Well, what did he write?"

I looked at the forlorn scrap clasped in my hand and read: "To Jackie, and I thank you for asking me. Bob Mitchum."

Now I knew it had all been worth it! He realized what my asking him had cost and he had responded with not only his name but a personal note as well, something *just* for me. And then a beautiful sense of pride enveloped me because, as scared as I was, I hadn't let my fears keep me from doing something that I had so desperately wanted to do.

Looking back now on that young self-conscious girl as she edged her way through such an intimidating maze of rough-hewn virility, I wanted to applaud her courage, and I thought he gave me something far more important than the thrill of that husky voice, the gaze of slow-movin' eyes and his name on a piece of paper—he gave me the chance to discover my own heroic stature.

BROWN SUGAR

SANDWICHES

By Brooke Anderson

It is strange that the first memory I have of meeting my grandmother is not of an extraordinary event. Odd how certain memories cling to us, hold us in a way that cannot be defined or explained.

My mother spent the middle part of the day dressing my six-year-old self in a navy blue cotton dress with a big oversized white pique collar that buttoned around the neckline. The dress tied in the back with a rather large bow. A little too frilly for the taste of my mother. The bow somehow made me feel pretty. My white socks were folded down two inches, just so, and tucked neatly into my white Maryjanes with a pearl button on each side. My mother fussed unreasonably with my hair so the part would be straight and brushed it under so the ends would not stick out. A natural colored straw hat with a navy ribbon glued around its perimeter covered up all her hard work. The worst part was the elastic band underneath my chin to hold the hat in place. It ate into my neck and seemed impossible to adjust. When I played with it, it would snap back causing a red smudge. I would sometimes take off the hat completely and tuck the elastic behind my ears but that itched my skin and I did not want to appear fidgety, not today, not while meeting my grandmother.

After a long, winding drive to my grandmother's rental house, my stomach a little queasy from rounding all the curves, we were greeted at the enormous front door by a houseman with oriental slippers who guided my mother and me through the entry. Quiet and shy he looked down at the ground as if there were something in the black and white marble floor that needed his attention. He led us into the living room. It was a vast space with large windows that magnified the world. I could see all of Los Angeles; buildings and sky, the ocean and Catalina just beyond the grasp of the thick white wool carpet and the elaborate furnishings. I was very nervous in the grand space. I felt a little bit like Stuart Little, smartly dressed but insignificant and needing to hide.

As my grandmother floated down the staircase her hand just above the black wrought iron banister she rang out, "Coming my darlings." Her floor length chiffon gown of tomato color was of great contrast to her head wrapped in a leopard turban. Real skins, before animal rights made us think. I could smell my grandmother as she entered the room. Cloves and carnations mixed with the richness of Joy perfume. We embraced. "Do sit down my precious ones," her deep voice was singing. We sat. I crossed my legs at the ankle as I had been instructed and just stared at her. Her hundreds of gold bracelets made clanking sounds as she hugged my mother. Sleigh bells as horses trotted through the snow, that was the sound. An out of place sound high in the Hollywood Hills with palm trees and heat and a Great Dane asleep in a wedge of sunlight.

Tea was set. Hot water in a sterling silver pitcher came out through a spigot. Silver tea strainers were placed over each china cup. The amber liquid poured through. Lots of milk and sugar was added to my cup. More milk than tea. "This is English style," my mother informed me. Thick slices of heavy, dank bread were displayed on a fluted crystal platter. A mound of saltless pale butter stood in a deep bowl next to a glass dish filled with dark brown sugar. My grandmother came over to the tiny white upholstered bench and sat down next to me. With a mother-of— pearl handled knife she spread butter on a piece of bread, then spooned brown sugar carefully on top and covered this mixture with another slice of bread. She placed the brown sugar sandwich on a flowered china dessert plate and cut it diagonally in half. "Here my little one." I took a bite. It was a strange sensation. The molasses hiding in the brown sugar was harsh and sweet at the same time. An extravagant taste.

The afternoon was getting late, the living room had darkened. No sun was left in the sky. My grandmother had to dress for the theater. She invited me upstairs. She changed into clothes that I had never before encountered. She removed from her closet a long black silk dress, strapless with a voluminous skirt and a huge diamond broach that tucked neatly in the bodice. She put on dark silk stockings and tiny black heels that she first allowed me to try on. They almost fit. Elbow length white kid gloves were placed on the counter top next to a long stemmed red carnation, a flower that she was never without. Her makeup had been set from earlier in the day. Her immense false dark eyelashes were glued permanently, it seemed, in place. After brushing her teeth with a powder that smelled of cinnamon, she traced her lips with a deep red pencil on top of which she applied a coat of crimson. She unwrapped the turban from her head and combed her dark hair until it was all fluffy and put on a hat trimmed in white ermine with a black lace veil. Over her bare shoulders she flung a mink stole that still had a head and tail intact.

I sat in wonder looking at my grandmother. A tiny, elegant woman who possessed a dramatic flare for dressing up. Her life on stage and in film added great mystery and intrigue as to who she really was. She floated in and out of my life on an irregular basis. Yet her beauty, curiosity, sense of style and independence formed me into knowing that I, too, could achieve whatever I wanted. From our very first encounter throughout her life she always listened intently with interest and without judgment.

I long for life to be simple again. To be absorbed in innocent pleasures. To be delighted by tea and her laughter and the flavor of something new and daring. I yearn to taste the bold sharpness of my grandmother's brown sugar sandwiches. Just one more time I want to sit in her company, to close my eyes while biting into the sweetness and dream of parties and friends and a prince and ponder what the future will hold.

THE PRAIRIE SAGE

By Dorothy Huebel

When there's a blizzard raging outdoors, there's only so much a house bound kid can do to keep busy. And I was a house bound kid. I'd cleaned my room, washed and ironed my dolls' clothes, read Little Men and Rose in Bloom, and worked on my "Patience is a Virtue" sampler until a french knot got tangled in a slip stitch and she, my mother, had no time to fix it. Of course not, she was in the basement helping my brother Donald build a ferris wheel with his erector set, or in the kitchen making brownies with nuts. She said she forgot to make half the pan without nuts but she knew darn well I'd choke if I had to eat nut strewn brownies.

I knew she'd hate it so I did it anyway. I rubbed the edge of my fist on the frosted window pane so I could watch the snow swirl and eddy in the grip of the wind before it fell to the snow drift that blocked our front door. I could just barely see through the white-out, but I thought I saw the outline of a figure plodding through the drifts and as it came closer, I could see it was a man with a bundle on his back and ill clad for a twenty degree below zero day. He rounded the corner of the house snapping off the wrist thick icicle that hung from the broken down spout as he walked around the back. His long hair and beard were white with snow, and his wet trousers and shirt front were plastered to his gaunt frame by the gale force winds. The only protection he had against the weather were mittened hands he held over his mouth and nose to keep his breath from freezing in his nostrils. Very soon I heard a knock on the back door.

My mother opened the door and a man yelled, "Ma'am, I'd be mighty grateful if you'd let me shovel a path to your front door in exchange for a bite to eat." She beckoned him in and said, "You can eat first and then shovel but take off your wet shoes and put them over there on the register to dry out." While she heated some soup and sliced the bread for sandwiches, he took off his shoes and I could see the cardboard patches covering the holes in the soles of those old worn out shoes.

Knowing my mother, I know how distressed she must have been at the thought of sending this man out doors without the clothing he needed to withstand the bitter weather. And I'm sure she asked herself where he and the hundreds of others like him, who during the depression crossed the country looking for work, slept while storms raged and temperatures dropped. I stayed in the kitchen while he ate and she went down to the basement.

I was really startled when he turned to me and said, "Miss Dorothy, it's mighty nice to see you again and how's your brother? You probably don't remember me but I met you and your Pa last summer down by the tracks where I was enjoying a breakfast of bacon and eggs with your brother and a couple of my pals. I often thought about how nice it was of your Dad not to run us off or to shame your brother in front of us." Sure I remembered him. I even remembered the three hobos with my brother and that this was the tall, skinny one who had been introduced as Clyde.

Mother came back upstairs carrying some of my dad's old clothes, a hunting jacket and a pair of goulashes that I suppose she took from the bag she kept for the town's annual rummage sale. "Go on down the cellar. You can wash up in the laundry tub and put on these clothes before I show you where the shovel is," she sort of mumbled and I knew she was worrying about what would happen to him at nightfall.

While he was in the basement I whispered to her that Clyde was an old friend of Donald's and that maybe Donald would like to visit with him. So, I suggested that she could ask him to have dinner with us when he finished shoveling and then maybe he could sleep on the cot in the basement storeroom. Our basement was divided into three separate rooms; the furnace room, the laundry room, and the storeroom where the family spent many a summer day escaping the 100 degree heat.

He washed, dressed, shoveled, ate dinner with us, slept on the cot in the basement storeroom and Donald was thrilled to have a companion. The next day Clyde fixed the sagging shelves in the laundry room where my mother kept the food she had put up during the summer, and she was thrilled to have that job done.

She said, "Every time I go down there I think I'm going to see the floor covered with broken mason jars and all of the fruit and jelly I canned." She was thrilled to have such a handyman around since it was the one attribute my father lacked.

Each day, until the storm was over, he shoveled the coal, banked the furnace, and hauled the ashes. And, he always found something to do around the house that needed doing. It seemed as if there wasn't anything he couldn't do. But, I know I wasn't really all that thrilled about having him there.

I got the feeling that my father wasn't either, at least until Bud, his building maintenance man, got sick and Clyde volunteered to work in his place. Before my father even let Clyde set foot in his work place he took him to Fowler's barbershop for a haircut and shave. I didn't change my mind until Clyde put a new front wheel on my balloon tire bicycle, and by then he had become a permanent member of our household.

Mother replaced the cot with a bed and she had him move an old dresser and desk from the attic to his basement lair. Somewhere he found a broken lamp that he repaired and he brought home a chair one of the tenants in my father's building had left behind. The storage room was now known as "Clyde's Room." He had a place to live. He had an address and soon he had a library card. He told me, "A library card is something I've wanted ever since I ran away from home years ago but I never had a permanent address 'til now."

Sometimes after dinner we'd all sit around the dining room table or if it was summer we'd sit out on the front porch listening to the band concert from the Court House lawn across the street and he'd tell us about the "U. S. of A" which he had traveled up and down and across, courtesy of the railroad system. Though he never told us why he left home or where he was from, the lilt and cadence of his voice suggested hillbilly but his vocabulary was that of a sage.

> "I'd just hop a freight, get off whenever I felt like it, or was chased off and if I liked the place and could find work, I'd stay a while and I learned something new with every job I ever had. You know, learning is really what gives spice to life. I've picked apples in Washington State and cotton down south. I was a wrangler on a Texas ranch, I worked in the steel mills in Pittsburgh and the stock yards in Chicago. I learned how to cook and to rope cattle, to shuck corn and pluck chickens, to weld, to fish, and to hunt. I can build a house or take one apart and I can fix just about anything. In every place I've been, if there was a library, I spent my spare time reading but I was never able to check out a book and take it home 'cause I didn't have a home to take it to. All I had was my tarp and a bed roll."

Every year when spring came, Clyde took down the storm windows and put up the screens. In the fall he reversed the procedure. He fixed the broken down spouts and emptied the mouse traps. He planted a vegetable garden out in back and he mowed the lawn. He beat the rugs and waxed the floors when my mother was spring-cleaning. He made the best fried chicken and Hobo stew I've ever had and he helped me lay out a pattern on some fabric I bought to make a dress for my Home Economics class assignment. I had skimped on the yardage but he showed me how to make the most of what I had and how to cut bias binding from the scraps and I never forgot it. He told me how fabric was made starting with the cotton balls through the ginning, carding, spinning, and weaving processes.

He had a steady job working for my father since Bud never fully recovered. Clyde did whatever needed to be done to keep the buildings in good repair. He ran the bingo game for the Boy Scouts during Corn Palace week, and when he walked down Main Street people greeted him by name. He'd found a place he liked and, as he said, "I aim to say put."

I don't remember when it was that he became a church-goer but one summer evening, when we were all out on the front porch, he told us that he was going to sit through the Sunday services in each of the Protestant churches until he found the one that had the best choir. And the best, in his opinion, was the Free Methodist church. And, that is where he met Emma, a widow woman whom he later married.

She was the organist and he loved to sing. As far as I know, Emma and Clyde lived happily ever after on the edge of town in her little farm house.

Clyde and Emma stayed with us when my folks went to Chicago for a week during my last year in high school. That was when Clyde explained to me why he thought I would be happier at the University of Wisconsin than the University of Minnesota, my two top choices.

> "I've lived a while in both places so I know that the U of M is just another enterprise to folks who live in Minneapolis. It's smack dab in the middle of a big city with heavy traffic, big buildings, lots of strangers and

distractions. It's too impersonal; it's just not your kind of
place. It's not so much that it's not for you; it's that
Wisconsin is your kind of place. Madison is a much
smaller town with kind of a homey feeling, and the
University is the heart and pride of the community. It's
the kind of place that invites contemplation, slakes the
thirst for knowledge and nurtures a sense of belonging."

I know those sound like awfully pretentious words but they
have become an indelible part of my memory of the Prairie Sage,
a wonderfully self sufficient man who appeared out of nowhere,
and by example, taught me how to live life.

CHAPTER TWO

Family

Writing about family members is a bit like cleaning out the closet, sorting and pressing the articles you want to maintain at the front of the closet to wear on special occasions and getting rid of the debris you don't need anymore. Every writer has at least one family member she loves and another who has brought great challenge into her life. When you write about your memory of a particular family member, it is your recollection, no one else's.

If your brother or sister would write their recollection of say, your great Aunt Harriet, she would probably be portrayed differently than yours. Not because you have lied or described her inaccurately, but because your experience of her is particular to you. You can check your memory of Aunt Harriet against your sibling's or child's or spouse's if you have one, but your emotional memory is still yours; at least until you write it down! I say that because when we write about a particular interpersonal relationship, we often find ourselves saying: "Did this really happen?" or "Did he really say that? No, he couldn't have said that, that's just too insensitive. But that's the way I remember it."

When Geoff Wolff wrote about his father and mother in *The Duke of Deception* and his brother Tobias Wolff wrote about that same father as well as his stepfather and mother in *This Boy's Life*, their mother threatened to write her own memoir. Geoff Wolff is reported to have said, "Go ahead, they're all true!" Truth is in the experience of the recollector.

In *Memories of a Catholic Girlhood*, Mary McCarthy writes that her great handicap as a memoirist is the fact that she was orphaned quite young and her chain of recollection—the collective memory of her family was broken with her parents' untimely death. She writes, "For events of my early childhood I have had to rely on my own sometimes blurry recollections, on the vague and contradictory testimony of uncles and aunts, on a few idle remarks of my grandmother's made before she became senile, and on some letters written me by a girlhood friend of my mothers."

What remains, however is her emotional memory, her memory of a grandmother to whom she was sent to live, who was as she describes, rather unpleasant. "I do not know how my Grandmother got the way she was; I assume, from family photographs and from the inflexibility of her habits, that she was always the same, and it seems as idle to inquire into her childhood as to ask what was ailing Iago or look for the error in toilet-training that was responsible for Lady Macbeth." McCarthy remembers her grandmother's indomitable will as the dominant trait of her nature.

The same could be said of Ruth Bochner's mother-in-law who refused to die in "Aphrodite Speaks." Bochner describes a woman who lingered way beyond her usefulness to herself and others; a woman who longed to die when her husband passed on and when she was denied that possibility, she wasted away for years thereafter. Bochner's piece is a powerful reminder of the universal feelings a daughter-in-law (or son-in-law) has about an aging in-law as she tries to avoid seeing the confused pain in her husband's eyes as she witnesses his spooning ice cream into his mother's mouth. Her voice is authentic; she writes the unspeakable thoughts of a much younger woman leaving the deathbed of the family matriarch.

"As we leave, escape to leaf-strewn path outside, I feel very young. I tightly tie the belt of my coat, and think, 'I am young, hardly worn, and I am strong, and my lips are red, and my shoes that crunch the leaves are shiny, black, smooth polished leather, and my husband, her son, is beside me, and we will have lunch now.'" She is not unkind; her words are true and insightful. Notice the detail of the ice cream that repeats in the piece.

Dorothy Huebel examines another perspective on truth in "Hierarchy of Deceit." With her great wit, Dorothy explores what to do with the volumes of unlabeled photographs of unknown ancestors left by her deceased mother.

"'It's a family heirloom to be passed from one generation to the next,' she said as she sighed and handed it to me. 'You're never really gone as long as someone remembers you.' So before

I handed it over to the next generation, I was compelled to make sure all the little black corners were securely glued and the photos properly identified."

I won't spoil the surprise of how Dorothy identifies the subjects of the photographs who will live on for her children and grandchildren or how she labels her own deceit, but her ingenuity will leave you wishing you had Dorothy's inventive imagination! Dorothy's piece about the "family hierloom" and "The Table" written by Marilyn Kierscey were both inspired by an assignment I gave the group to write about an artifact or family object.

Marilyn Kierscey writes with great detail and emotional warmth about the dining room table passed down to her from her Grandma which has actively participated in family gatherings giving succor, protection, and witness to the rites of passage performed by four generations. "My parents announced their engagement at the table, and their wedding cake was the centerpiece one hot Saturday afternoon in July 1942." A few months after her own marriage, Marilyn sat down at the table with her Grandma. "'I'm going to have a baby,' I told her. 'My stars, doesn't seem so long ago that you were sitting right next to me in a high chair,' she said.'"

The table remains a constant for Marilyn as family members leave their place at the table to move on with their own lives, or in some cases, death or divorce. The food changes, the center piece of flowers changes with the seasons, but the memories and spirit of the family, particularly of Marilyn's Grandma, remains.

As you read the pieces in this section, remember to look for the elements of memoir writing and think about what object or artifact would conjure up your own family memories and how you would enter into the same or a similar subject.

THE TABLE

By Marilyn Kierscey

When the last big earthquake shook our Southern California home, I grabbed my cat and crawled under our dining room table. "Snookums," I whispered "we'll be safe here." Four generations of my family had hidden under the table during earthquakes. No one had ever been injured.

My grandparents bought the table from a family who had lost their money in the 1929 stock market crash and needed cash quickly. My grandparents needed a big, solid dining table. In addition to their six children, relatives and friends often joined them for meals.

The long, low windows of the dining room opened on the front garden. The scent of roses and freshly mown grass drifted into the room. Sunlight streamed in and fell on the mahogany table with its carved legs and feet.

Grandma picked her fresh flowers for the centerpiece. The daffodils and sweet peas of spring were my favorites. She kept the table uncovered except for meals. She wanted us to enjoy its beauty.

"A home cooked meal fixes whatever ails a person," she said while baking bread, making strawberry jam, or cooking pot roast. My uncles' friends, including members of the scrawny, often defeated UCLA football team of the late 1930's, enjoyed her Sunday dinners. She hoped her meals would fatten up the football players and improve their chances of winning some games.

No one rushed away after eating, but stayed to join in the conversations. My aunts and uncles talked about their college classes, where Glen Miller and his band were playing next, and the war in Europe.

My parents announced their engagement at the table, and their wedding cake was the centerpiece one hot Saturday afternoon in July 1942.

During World War II, while three of my uncles fought in Europe and the Far East, their wives lived with my grandparents. They shared their rationed food and their worries. The spaces where my uncles normally sat were kept empty until they returned.

After the war, the grandchildren came, twelve of us all together. Teeth marks showed on the carved legs where we gnawed as babies. On rainy days when we were older, we draped Grandma's ironed sheets over the table, making it our secret house or our pirate ship.

Soon we were expected to sit in our chairs and listen. My Uncle Francis, proclaiming himself a liberal by wearing a pink shirt, declared that Franklin Roosevelt saved the country. My Uncle Malc shouted, "Absolutely not. FDR started it on the path to ruin." Each adult presented his or her opinion as being the One Truth. I didn't know which truth was the one truth. Since they all sounded convincing, I took a bit from each one and formed my own opinions.

After the men left the table, the women leaned their elbows on its edges. Their voices whispered with secrets. I tried to listen, but my cousins and I were sent to the kitchen to help Grandpa wash and dry the dishes.

I was ten when my Uncle Bob, my mother's youngest brother, died. He returned from fighting in France and Germany with a hero's medals and with deep emotional wounds. I overheard hushed, sad conversations between my mother and my grandmother. No one knew how to treat war veterans who trembled and dived for cover when noises reminded them of the sounds of bombs or gunfire.

For a year after he died, my grandmother cried through every family meal. The next spring when she arranged daffodils and lilacs for the centerpiece, we knew she was better. But my uncle's place remained empty. I grew up believing it was bad luck to sit there.

During college, when I needed love and a home-cooked meal, I took the bus from UCLA to my grandparents' house. They greeted me as if they'd been waiting just for me. At one meal, Grandpa said, "You look peaked. Why not try my coffee?" I sipped my first cup of coffee, then another, and another. He made coffee so strong that I didn't sleep at all that night. The day I graduated from UCLA, Grandma fixed a special lunch and gave me a thick dictionary and Amy Vanderbilt's *New Complete Book of Etiquette*.

A few months after my marriage, Grandma and I sat down at the table. "I'm going to have a baby," I told her. "My stars, doesn't seem so long ago that you were sitting right next to me in a high chair," she said.

My son, Shawn, was her sixth great grandchild.

After Grandpa died, she moved to a small apartment with no room for the table. She loaned it to me for our family Thanksgiving dinner. "Grandma, I'll help you to your seat," I said while guiding her to her customary place.

"No." She shook her head. "You sit here tonight."

Shawn's first birthday dinner was celebrated around the table. Six months later, it was loaded in a van when Shawn and I moved to an apartment and I filed for divorce.

When my grandmother died, my mother wanted me to have the table permanently. With my life feeling broken except for Shawn, I didn't feel it belonged with me. But I wouldn't give it up. I cut out dress patterns, sewed curtains, wrote my first children's story, and typed my master's thesis on its surface.

Having it carried up one hundred steps to one apartment made me wonder. Why was I holding onto such a cumbersome piece of furniture? It moved eight times with my son and me. Its solidity held me when I felt fragile. It helped me believe a better time would come.

My second husband and I bought a house with no separate dining room, only a small area off the kitchen. "Ted, I know my table will fit there."

"Absolutely, not," he said. "That's the worst idea I've heard." For three days, we fought. When he left for a few hours, I asked a friend to help me. We pulled and pushed and finally moved it. After it was in place, Ted was delighted with the way it fit.

A year ago we celebrated Shawn's graduation from college with a dinner around the table. He talked of wanting to marry and have children. I hope in a few years there will be a high chair and the sounds of a baby or two, a fifth generation to join us. When they are older, I can show them the teeth marks my cousins and I made as toddlers.

Sometimes when it's quiet, I can almost hear Grandma's loud sighs waiting for Grandpa's long grace to be over so we could eat. He always ended with the words, "Thank you, God, for our family, for those gathered here and those with us in our hearts."

APHRODITE SPEAKS

By Ruth Bochner

Why do I feel just this moment a door closing on my mother-in-law who died on the twenty-eighth? Why do I think of beauty and sensuality and feel a prickle of fear, of disconsolate unrest, or apprehension? Not on the twenty-eighth, but now.

My mother-in-law died five years ago and traded her being life for one of a breathing cadaver. My daughter claimed, "If only Dad would give her permission to die—she would." "You do it then," I said. "He wouldn't know how."

But I tried through the years, as I fed her a paper cup of ice cream from a flat wood spoon, repulsed but marveling as the mouth opened for the treat, like a baby sparrow. "It's okay to die," I whispered to both of us. "You're finished here. Your hard-earned money down the drain for sitters in this joyless room, this chronic-care place that keeps you dead-alive, alive-dead, and moves and washes and tucks you in to sterile comfort.

But you are not ready. Are you here to remind us that the body is a machine needing care and lubrication, imprisoned in this little being that was once so tall and vibrant? You arrogantly refused it that. It was your desire to die when Charlie died, like suttee in India, to throw yourself on the pyre like a devoted wife, selfless, worthless to self and the world without your man. You were vital, to be reckoned with. Alas, now there is no steel rod running through your spine.

When they took you away there was only tea and ice cream in that stone and stucco Tudor house you insisted was full of memories—the ashes of a life. We saw you only three days before you died. You were the same; crouched in a fetal position, gray parchment tightly stretched over your tiny bones, lifeless.

The same ice cream. "You feed her," I said to her son and busied myself as always with counting bed jackets and nighties. Counting and busying so that I would not have to see the confused pain in his eyes. "Does she weigh forty pounds?" he asked, pressing his fingers on her bony shoulders. I answered, "Oh about sixty, she's out of Nivea, I'll get it at the gift shop," knowing that the shop was closed on Sunday morning.

I escaped to walk the halls to find a nurse as always, to thank her for the care. This was a rich-voiced Jamaican with a broad smile. "Where's Lloyd?" she asked. "In the room," I answered. "How is it possible that she's still alive?" She shrugged, "We don't understand either." "How can you do this kind of work?" A shrug. "We're good at it," she answered.

I leave to go back. She comes to the room to see Lloyd, to bring a bib, to ask about California, why he is here and for how long. Does she wonder how this shriveled half corpse can have a tall, absent son. I hand the nurse the box of candy; I murmur, "God love you people." It's always the same. "Is it four years or five?" I ask Lloyd. A sigh. "What difference?" he answers.

As we leave, escape to leaf-strewn path outside, I feel very young. I tightly tie the belt of my coat, and I think, "I am young, hardly worn, and I am strong, and my lips are red, and my shoes that crunch the leaves are shiny, black, smooth polished leather, and my husband, her son, is beside me, and we will have lunch now. A warming lunch with wine, and I will feel glad that she is someone else's mother, and that I am hardly worn and can sniff the bite in the fall air, and I will feel rich, powerful, superior, as the car speeds away and tomorrow I will be home in Los Angeles, and I will not have to come back here for months and relive it all again, this deadly scene."

The call came Tuesday night.

"To be expected," I heard him say.

"Over due," I whispered.

HIERARCHY OF DECEIT

By Dorothy S. Huebel

I am a neat and orderly person, a bit compulsive, and until recently, known to be incorruptible. My spices are alphabetized, socks paired, recipes filed, and spoons nested. I turn my mattress the first Monday of every month, and I only cross an intersection at the "walk" sign. I'm a linear thinker, and the following hierarchy of deceit is an example of my tendency toward incrementalized thinking. In this case I started with the least offensive of the possibilities and moved on from there.

LEVEL OF DECEIT	EXAMPLE
1. DISSEMBLING	"You've never looked better."
2. FIBBING	"I wish I could, but I'm having out of town guests."
3. LYING	"I don't care what the sales slip says, I bought it yesterday."
4. PREVARICATING	"I promise to love, honor, and obey until death do us part."

I'll admit I've been guilty on occasion of dissembling and

fibbing, but lying and prevaricating are not my wont, but it was a photo album that nearly lured me from the straight and narrow path of truth.

It wasn't even my album, it was my Mother's. "It is a family heirloom to be passed from one generation to the next," she said as she sighed and handed it to me. "You're never really gone as long as someone remembers you." So, before I handed it over to the next generation, I was compelled to make sure all the little black corners were securely glued and the photos properly identified. Unfortunately, I had no idea who most of the photographed subjects were.

I had no problem recognizing my mother as a young child, an adolescent, a bride and a parent. I could easily identify my maternal and paternal grandparents. And, since my father and brother looked alike, and I knew the boy in the rompers, knickers, Boy Scout outfit, baseball uniform and the cap and gown was my brother, I assumed, that the baby in the arms of my paternal grandmother, the lad in overalls with a soup bowl haircut, and the young man in the World War I uniform were one and the same—my father. Of course I could identify my own baby picture, but I had no idea who all the other asexual, hairless, toothless, look-alike infants were.

I was at a loss when I looked through the pages of pictures of young women in long, flowery lace trimmed dresses, reticules, parasols, and feathered hats, bobbed hair, fringed dresses, and high heel shoes, maidens in middy blouses, or skirted bathing costume and ruffled caps teasing the ripples at the edge of an unnamed lake. I found duplicate prints of a lass in a buttoned up, linen coat, called a duster and a veiled bonnet with a dashing youth in goggles and a cap leaning against the running board of a Packard phaeton. And, there were dozens of snaps of young, middle aged and older men in three-piece suits with watch fobs stretched across their vests standing, sitting, kneeling, waving, all of them with their faces obscured by the brims of their felt fedoras. Interspersed, as if to add to the confusion, were photographs taken at weddings, birthday parties, graduations, and baby naming ceremonies, but there was not a clue as to whose wedding, birthday, graduation or baby naming ceremony had been memorialized in those little, 3"x4" black and white pictures with their pinked borders.

Crestfallen, but undaunted, I tackled the problem and solved it in my own way. Logic suggested that some of the unidentified had to be my parents' siblings, their spouses and look-alike infants. Compulsion suggested that I make a list of all the aunts, uncles and cousins I could remember. Though I'd never met them I heard my mother talk about her first through twelfth grade classmates in Sioux City, Iowa, Nettie and Bess, so I just added a few more generation-appropriate given names to fill out the list, in case they were needed for the group pictures. It was deceit, however, that suggested I type each name listed on little slips of the yellowed paper I found in her diary and paste a named slip beneath each photo, and that is what I did.

Having embraced deceit, I can now sit, knit, and listen to my daughter talk to her daughter, as they turn the pages of the family heirloom, "Look, that's my great aunt Tillie and Uncle Harry's wedding picture. Him? Are you looking at the cowboy with the pitchfork in his hand? He's my grandfather's brother, Dave. Those people? You mean the man and woman leaning on the car? She's my grandma's best friend Nettie and that's her boy friend Wilbur. That group picture was taken at my great grandparents' fiftieth wedding anniversary, and the six people in the front row are their children: Fannie, Bessie, Nell, Gertie, Sam, and Lennie. No, Sweetie, that's not my baby picture, it says right here that's my mother's cousin Billie, the eldest son of Shirley, the daughter of my grandmother's sister Goldie."

True, the process required an admission of corruptibility and a slight adjustment in my code of ethics. On the other hand, I believe I dealt with the situation in a compulsively neat and orderly fashion. I reconfigured my hierarchy of deceit. All I had to do was slot "Familial Fabrication" right after fibs and before lies. To my way of thinking FF is just a tad more deceitful than fibbing, not as sinful as lying and has none of the flagrant "in your face" flavor of a prevarication. Though what I did lays bare a character flaw, it was worth a blot on my escutcheon. Now, may my mother rest in peace. Neither she nor any of her friends and family members are really gone, for they will be long remembered, just as I've identified them.

CHAPTER THREE

Mothers

"We most of our adult lives trying to grasp the meaning of our parents' lives; and how we shape and answer these questions largely turn us into who we are."

Phillip Lopate

The relationship with one's mother is always complex no matter whether she is supportive and loving, overbearing and clingy, distant or remote. Best selling books such as Frank McCourt's *Angela's Ashes*, James *McBride's The Color of Water*, and Jackie Lyden's *The Daughter of the Queen of Sheba* are just three of the full-length contemporary memoirs that have explored the deep desire the memoirist has to understand the motivations of his or her mother and to accept or undo her ever-present influence in their lives.

Sweet confections serve to focus two of the pieces in this section on mothers. In "A Cake Made of Dreams," Ruth Bracken uses her mother's strawberry shortcake recipe and her mother's preparation of it on the night before Ruth's wedding to illustrate her relationship with her mother. In my piece, "Riddles," a tin of Nanaimo bars made by my daughter sweetens her announcement of becoming a mom. Dorothy Huebel tries to reckon with her mother's haunting nagging voice over an afternoon glass of Beefeater's, so it looks like the concept of mothering is synonymous with nourishment or the lack thereof!

Ruth places her piece in the cultural context of the late 1960s, a time of anti-war protests, youthful idealism, backpacking to foreign continents, working on communes, and spontaneous marriages. When Ruth and her soon-to-be twenty-something husband return home from their Kubbutz near the Golan border to be married in her divorced mother's sunny California backyard, Ruth begs her mother to make her favorite cake for the wedding. Her mother responds:

"We'll go to Hansen's Bakery. Maybe they can do a layer

cake by Saturday." My mother rubbed her right cheek, a habit I knew well.

"Mom, you know that won't work. You have to make your shortcake. Nothing else comes close."

"It's a dessert roll," she interrupted firmly. "Not a shortcake."

This short dialogue gives the reader a hint of the tug-of-war between mother and daughter about to ensue. Ruth has a deft hand with both dialogue and description and never hesitates to implicate herself as well as others with her poignant humor. She is also a fabulous baker; when Ruth first read "Cake Made of Dreams" to our writing group, we were all savoring a piece of her freshly made strawberry dessert roll. She's right; nothing else comes close!

"Riddles" has a twist; it is about a daughter nourishing a mother as she herself moves into a new stage in life. I originally wrote this piece as a narrative poem in the second person addressed to my then twenty-eight year old daughter, Heather. Most memoirs are written in the first person narrative, past tense although some memoirists are very successful at achieving more intimacy by writing in first person, present tense. Others, like Vivian Gornick in her memoir about her mother, *Fierce Attachments*, are masters at changing tense within the same piece, even within the same paragraph. But I don't advise you to try that until you are skillful with one. Writing in the second person "letter" form has an interesting effect; it draws the reader into the immediate emotions of the situation.

In The Way Forward is with a Broken Heart, Alice Walker writes her memoir of a marriage to the husband of her youth, from whom she has been divorced for two decades.

> "You do not talk to me now, a fate I could not have imagined twenty years ago. It is true we say the usual greetings, when we have to, over the phone: How are you? Have you heard from Our Child? But beyond that,

really nothing. Nothing of the secrets, memories, good
and bad, that we shared."

As a reader, perhaps remembering your own young marriage,
you are drawn into the bittersweet feelings of her loss. Perhaps
you have been there too, or your sister, or your son; and you
recall all the tender hopes and dreams shared by young
newlyweds. That is the poignancy of memoir; it reminds us of
ourselves.

"Riddles" explores the mixed emotions a middle-aged mother
feels when she first hears that she will become a grandmother
and fears she will be replaced in her daughter's heart by the new
life that now grows within her womb. But that type of loss, as her
daughter moves to take her rightful place in the mother line of
her relations, cannot be expressed in the midst of such joyful
tidings. The paradox of delight and grief is experienced by the
writer alone and saved for later reflection. She is too busy fending
off her daughter's frustration that she guessed her riddle too soon!

In "Platitudes on the Rocks," Dorothy Huebel describes one
of those very bad days when everything, but everything, goes
wrong and you can do nothing to quiet your mother's inner voice.
No matter how long she's been deceased or how much you argue
with that voice, your mother's dictums can not be silenced. "Idle
hands are the devil's workshop," "Haste makes waste," "Pride
goeth before a fall."

We all have our favorites and they come back to haunt us at
the most maddening times. Using colloquialisms in memoirs, if
not overdone, is always encouraged; they immediately place a
character in historical time and temperament.

Students sometimes say, "Nothing significant ever happens
to me. What am I going to write about?" And I answer, "No event
is insignificant if you can mine it for understanding of your loved
ones and insight about yourself." Dorothy takes a rather ordinary
day and describes her interaction with the voice beyond the grave

with such precise detail and hilarity that the reader can easily sympathize with her remedy of two fingers of gin! I wonder how you would tackle the writing of a similar remembered event.

A CAKE MADE OF

DREAMS

By Ruth Bracken

My mother's strawberry shortcake was the only dessert she made with elegance, and the only one I'd eat. In fact, it wasn't a shortcake at all. The precise name was "dessert roll," a word my mother insisted upon. Shortcake or roll: either term didn't really describe something made of air. Sweet summer air, studded with the reddest of fruit, dressed with the lightest of cream. A cake made of dreams; nothing else would do for the wedding, even on short notice.

Bill and I had returned to Los Angeles only one week before our wedding. We were dirty and weary from three months on the road, hitchhiking Europe, looking for Utopia. Like a number of students caught in the confusion of the sixties, I had fled the uncertainty and violence of Berkeley, while Bill had come along for the ride—and to follow me, perhaps. I needed a lot of distance from certain memories: the sight of uniformed young men from the National Guard charging into my dance studio, their thick black boots scuffing the polished floors, guns pointed and ready;

my dance teacher, a human metronome continuing his irreversible "One, two and three;" surrealistic clouds of poison surrounding People's Park; staring up at the rounded base of a wooden club, inches from my own head. By late spring of 1969, nothing made sense and everything was too loud, smoky and dangerous.

I had hoped that a journey to an older, wiser part of the world might reveal what I could do with my life—besides dancing away from tear gas. But the expedition Bill and I made was far from a grand waltz through Europe on twenty bucks a day. Instead, we specialized in youth, idealism and discomfort. We were searching for a community or some version of it, blindly progressing from hitchhiking in the rain outside of Belfast to surviving snow in a workcamp just south of the Arctic Circle in Norway. By late August we ended up picking pears on a blistering kibbutz in Israel. It took a long-distance call to my mother, during which jets screamed overhead constantly, to realize the extent of our extremes.

"What's that noise I hear?" my mother yelled into the receiver.

"Oh, the bombers, I guess," I shouted back.

"What bombers? Where are you?"

"Bet Kachet. Remember, I wrote you. A kibbutz near the Golan border. We were hoping to work here with the children, but they make you pick pears for the first six months to see if you're serious."

"Serious? But what about the jets? Are you in any danger?"

"A seven-day war that's lasting a . . ."

"Get the hell out of there—now! Do the two of you have no sense at all? I didn't send you to the best schools so that you could . . ."

Our connection broke off, but the gist of my mother's angst echoed in the sun-baked telephone conference room.

"What are we doing here, Bill?" I turned to my companion. "I've had enough pears and desert to last my lifetime. Let's go home."

"Had enough pears?" He stopped for a moment, looking down at his hands. I had met Bill in Berkeley at an encounter group, one of the hilarious inventions of those soul-searching times. But baring one's soul to a small group of strangers proved to be a good way to get a date. Bill's mixture of honesty and ironic intelligence frightened and attracted me in equal measure. I tried to ignore him; he saw right through me, a human x-ray machine.

Two weeks after the group began, Bill showed up on my doorstep dismissing my current boyfriend with an easy smile. In the year we lived together, we had survived my mother's first stroke on hearing of our communal status, followed by her disowning and reluctant reclaiming of me as her only daughter. My inexperience and a certain sense of trembling whenever my dance professor began to roar, required substantial support, which amazingly I received from Bill. In time, we both grew used to each other.

As I waited for Bill to speak I looked out the solitary dusty screen of our temporary Israeli home and realized I had learned to love by watching him. Especially when he was quiet, rotating the large school ring on his ring finger. Usually he was thinking, often about things that would change my own life.

"Want to go home and get married?" Bill asked me then, casually. "Your mom would probably like that a lot. Get her to cool down a bit." It was my turn to be quiet, but not for long.

"Wow. Sounds like a great idea to me. Get out of this parched place of pears. California, here we come." I reached up to ruffle the back of Bill's black springy curls, and look into his green eyes. Their brown flecks held me steadily. After I hugged him hard, I stepped outside to wave good-bye to Israel.

We both started packing within the hour. I remember studying the length and width of my ring finger, considering the weight of a ring.

Two weeks later, Bill and my mother and I sat in the small breakfast nook of her kitchen, discussing wedding plans. The suddenness of our return, coupled with a wedding caused my mother to double her ration of cigarettes until she was chain smoking day and night.

"We'll go to Hansen's Bakery. Maybe they can do a layer cake by Saturday." My mother rubbed her right cheek, a habit I knew well.

"Mom, you know that won't work. You have to make your shortcake. Nothing else comes close," I pleaded.

"It's a dessert roll," she interrupted firmly. "Not a shortcake."

"Whatever. What would we want with one of those horrid towers of white sugar, topped with a petrified man in a tight suit and his frozen bride in fake tulle?" I asked her.

My mother's lips folded together in a tight line, the way they did when she had much to say and no one who would listen to her.

"Come on, Mom. I'm doing all the other cooking; you won't have to do one other thing, I promise. We'll even clean up."

"I'm sure. Who is we?" My mother's eyebrows and voice rose in an unpleasant sing-song of skepticism. "You and Bill will be sniffing your leis before you even remember the dirty dishes in the kitchen."

One disadvantage of a mother is that she knows you too well.

"Well, you're the one who bought us the tickets to Hawaii for the very next morning after the wedding," I reminded her.

"I'd rather have you looking for Utopia in Hawaii than in Israel. You guys are going to have to get jobs there right away, you know," my mother's voice trailed off into another warning.

"Mom, please don't lecture me now. We were talking about the wedding, for god's sake." I tried another tactic. "Are you telling me you're not going to bake the best cake in the whole world, and the only one I'll eat, just because you have too much to do?"

I heard her late that night in the kitchen. Pulling out the dusty jelly roll pan from the rarely opened cabinet. Cleaning out the Mixmaster, cursing the daddy long-legs crawling out of the beaters. Pushing aside the aluminum foil in the junk drawer, searching for the long roll of wax paper.

"What's your mother doing?" Bill groaned. The guest bedroom, six feet from the kitchen, was not soundproofed.

"Shhh. She's baking the cake. Don't spoil anything now." I put my hand over his mouth. He bit it.

"She's starting to bake the wedding cake at 11:00 p.m?"

I shrugged in the dark. "She's always been like this. Comatose before 11:00 a.m., and in full swing by midnight."

"So she's going to cook all night?"

I nodded, and pulled myself up on the pillows. "Yeah, probably. This cake is a lot of work. Tons of steps. Takes forever. It's the only thing she never let me help her with. So I'm not exactly sure how long it takes. But wait until you taste it."

"Worth it?" my future husband asked.

"Did the sun rise? Are there big waves in Hawaii?"

"That good, huh?" I heard him smiling. "Guess we better get your mom a ton of fresh strawberries tomorrow."

"Great idea." I hugged him. "We can go to the Farmer's Market early in the morning."

I recall these pictures of the wedding: a polished silver dish half-full of neatly rolled joints; bottles of champagne popping; a rabbi-for-hire who improvised the service, then babbled on while Bill frowned at him; several disturbed squirrels, dropping avocados on the guests like enormous green turds; my mother's longest table set with fresh salads, two kinds of sprouts, sliced fruits, three kinds of homemade breads and the only thing I ate: my mother's strawberry dessert roll. A cake made of dreams.

RIDDLES

By Maureen Murdock

You meet me on the bluffs
overlooking the wild ocean
in Santa Cruz
next to Natural Bridges
where you took me to see the Monarch Butterflies
that first long autumn of your freshman year.
The year I cried myself to sleep each night
in your empty childhood bed.

You have driven South
from San Francisco
where you live with your husband.
I have driven North
from Santa Barbara where I now live alone.
We arrive at the same moment
both thrilled by our timing.
We smile that we are wearing
identical sage green sweatshirts
I ordered for us
from, of all places,
Victoria Secret's catalogue.

"Are you hungry, Mom, would you like to eat?
Or could we go for a walk?"
I'm hungry but I know you
are looking forward to Aragona's pizza for dinner
and to feast your eyes on the sea.
We walk south stretching our legs,
exchanging news, swapping gossip.
You have come to spend the night with me
in the mountains
at an international women writers' retreat
where I am scheduled to speak.

The winter wind blows your long black hair
away from your face.
It stirs your ruddy complexion pink
and your eyes cobalt blue.
Two nights ago I dreamed
your hand held the hand of a wee one.
She had the jet-black curls
of your very first year

We walk past couples strolling,
bikers pedaling, a statue of a woman
I had never seen before.
"Mom, I have something for you,"
as you proffer a tin.
My daughter the pastry chef, with some new confection.
Nanaimo bars, I hope, as I quicken to the memory
of a chocolate and peanut butter Pender Island summer
when you were sixteen and garnered
the recipe early one morning from a long lost friend.

I start to lift the lid but your voice stays my hand.
"Read the card first, Mom,"
you say with a grin.

Not a birthday or holiday to celebrate,
I look at you quizzically.
But I know it must be a riddle;
You've loved word games
since you were young.

"What's small and pink and soft all over,
has a long ripening period but is perfect in October?"
I stop reading and look up to take all of you in.
The flash from your camera freezes
the wonder on my face.
"How do you know you're having a girl?" I ask.
You are impatient. You stamp your foot.
I have spoiled your surprise.
I have guessed the pregnant riddle.

"You have to read further, Mom,
finish the whole rhyme."
I comply but I travel to image trapped by time.
This is not my dream daughter
holding her dark-haired daughter's hand.
No, this is my flesh-and-blood daughter
who is going to give birth to her very first child!

I pause, baffled by the sequence of my emotions
poignant loss, wonder,
excitement all rolled into one
I am too young to be a grandmother,
I rebel inside
I will no longer be your favorite female
Another will claim your heart and soul.
I will be displaced. You will be Mother
And the curly headed tot will call you Moma.

But you see nothing of this
Because I whoop with delight,
Kick up my heels
and tearfully hold you close to me.
I look into your eyes and see
the love that is blind
with the new heart that already beats
deep within.

PLATITUDES ON THE

ROCKS

By Dorothy S. Huebel

At exactly 2:48 p.m. on a sunny Wednesday in September, as I poured myself two fingers of Beefeaters gin over an ice cube, sat down in my favorite chair, put an ice pack on my twisted ankle, and removed the bloody band aid from my index finger, I heard that maternal voice from beyond whispering: "Idle hands are the devil's workshop."

> "I know, that's why I'm using both hands to hold the glass, and by the way, I got your message. The curtains have been washed."

I can still see her frowning as she stood on the back porch and impaled every inch of her lace curtains on the little nails sticking out of an adjustable rectangular wooden contraption.

I prefer Tangueray, but the bottle of Beefeaters was easier to reach. It's not as if I never before had a mid-day drink, but when I did, it was for business reasons or some other special occasion that called for celebration—like my retirement. And, my husband and I always had a drink or two after work and before I started dinner to give me time to unwind and change roles, a two-martini costume change from boss to housewife. When I became a full time housewife with a one-role wardrobe, and the doctor reminded me that liquor is nothing but empty calories, I gave it up. Who in their right mind would choose two hundred calories of booze instead of a very small brownie with a dab of vanilla ice cream? So, the fact that I finished my first drink and had a second at three o'clock that September afternoon was unusual, but I'd do it again given the same or similar circumstances.

My kitchen/breakfast room has five windows, each festooned with a pair of dotted swiss curtains with each little dot designed to be a magnet for culinary effluvia which turns white curtains limp and yellow. I don't even listen to that voice any more when it intrudes to remind me cleanliness is next to Godliness because I always wash the curtains right after the Jewish New Year and before the day of atonement.

So, at nine o'clock on that sunny September morn, I got out the step-stool, took the curtains down, put them in the washing machine and while they were in the dryer, I washed the windows inside and out, and cleaned the window frames and screens. Then I set up the ironing board, spray starched, and ironed the little eyelet-trimmed ruffles when I noticed that one of the ruffles was no longer stitched to the curtains. Having heard a thousand times that a stitch in time saves nine, I turned off the iron and got out my sewing kit. I had no problem finding the white thread and a needle. "Everything in its place and a place for everything," she always said.

It wasn't easy, but eventually I did thread the needle, and as I took the first stitch, I punctured the index finger of my left hand. It was a tiny puncture wound, but from the amount of blood that raced from one Swiss dot to the next on the freshly washed and ironed curtain, it might as well have been an incision. I reached for a towel to staunch the flow, but what I grabbed was another of the ready to hang curtains. Now I had two bloody curtains.

I had just put the curtains in a pail of cold water when I remembered I had letters to mail, and glancing out the window I saw the mailman approaching the house. I grabbed the letters, and as I walked out the front door to meet him the door blew shut. I was locked out of my own house. Though I tried, I couldn't climb the wall, I couldn't jimmy the driveway gate lock, but I could put a brick through a window if I could find a brick and a window I could climb through. By the time I found the brick, my neighbor with a key to my house came home and I was back in the kitchen.

I washed, dried, and ironed the two curtains, and since I couldn't hold a needle with my injured hand and thread it with my right, I opted to pin the flounce in place. I had those little gold safety pins in my hand when I heard that oft repeated admonition: "Sew it, young lady, do not pin it. What if you were in an accident and someone saw you lying on the ground with your slip strap held in place with a safety pin?" Who am I to tempt fate? I managed to thread the needle, sew the ruffle back in place, and thanked the Lord that I no longer wore slips, not even half-slips. No pins would be seen in my kitchen curtains by anyone lurking outside the window looking for a reason to talk about me.

Once again I mounted the step stool, put the curtains on the rods, and slipped the rods on their little metal hooks. Looking up I smiled, and stepping down I missed the bottom rung of the ladder. So much for anything worth doing is worth doing well. My twisted ankle hurt as I limped to the refrigerator, my needle-punctured finger throbbed, and my sense of joy in a job well done was seriously wounded. It's not necessarily true that pride goeth before a fall, mine went after I'd fallen. But, I had enough presence of mind to reach for an ice cube, an ice pack and the chilled glass I use for iced tea. Then I hobbled to the liquor cabinet and grabbed the Beefeaters.

Please don't say, "Time heals all wounds," because being a dutiful and loving daughter I would have to answer, "Mother, you are absolutely right, but on a lovely Wednesday in September at exactly 2:48p.m., a good stiff drink is better. No, I don't want to argue with you, but weren't you the one who said, "Time flies when you're having fun?"

CHAPTER FOUR

Fathers

"For I have always known that I lived at the center of the
heart of a passionate man."

Mary Gordon, *Shadow Man*

The relationship with the father is no less complex than the
relationship with the mother, but for daughters it is more covert.
Whether your father has been adored, idealized, a bully, or
absent, Father is a huge presence in any woman's life and
memoirists are writing about the multi-faceted relationship with
dear old dad. Mary Gordon sets out to sort out the contradictory
identities of her father who died when she was seven in *Shadow
Man* and in *The Bookmaker's Daughter*, Shirley Abbot seeks to
separate from her idealized southern father for whom she lived
her intellectual life. In *Daddy, We Never Knew You*, Germaine
Greer goes in search over three continents for the father who
never returned whole from fighting in the second World War and
Jenny Kiski writes about her fantasy father, Danny Kaye, in
Skating to Antarctica.

Each memoirist in this section explores a different aspect of
the father-daughter relationship with great emotional truth. Bairbre
Dowling has an actor's ear for dialogue. She opens her piece, "I
Called my Father Vincent," with the sound of her father's voice:
"'This is my sleeping time,' he roared sitting bolt upright in the
mahogany marriage bed. It happened almost every time I forgot
to get the hairbrush. The loudness in the darkened room, the
furious tone, the edge to his voice stopping me in my creeping
tracks, right under the gold framed picture of their marriage
certificate signed by the Pope or some big Bishop in Rome."

Notice the emotional tone Bairbre sets immediately, not only
through her father's roar but also the details of the darkened
room.

"'Sorry Vin,' I whisper trying to return the bedroom to its
predisturbed state. 'I just need to get the hairbrush.' I inch my

way toward the velvet-curtained bay window as he thumps his pillow in exasperation, huffing and puffing."

Bairbre's "inching" in and out of the room while her father expresses his displeasure through thumping and hrumping adds to the immediate dramatic tension of this piece. Memoir needs drama and insight to qualify as a memoir and Bairbre invites the reader into the drama of a very intimate moment. She ends up letting her father off the hook for his cross words as many daughters do (with a man they both love and fear), but the reader knows the writer is wise beyond words about who this father truly is.

Dorothy Huebel describes the adulation a five-year-old girl has for her father as hero: "He was bigger than the colossus of Rhodes, braver than Sitting Bull, stronger than Sampson, better looking than Ramon Navarro, and wiser than Solomon." The event Dorothy remembers to illustrate her father's heroics is the stuff of small town lore. Her father, a Republican, rented office space to an aspiring Democrat by the name of George McGovern. Dorothy's incisive wit shines through as she describes the reaction of the local Republican women: "The next morning the officers of the Republican Women's Club marched down main street in full regalia, which in those days meant hats and white gloves. They flew in the front door of my father's store like a covey of geese headed north and demanded an explanation." You'll have to read on to find out how Dorothy's father resolved the complaint but once again Dorothy sets her piece within a historical context and the reader is richer for her attention to details.

Bairbre uses dialogue skillfully and Dorothy uses historical context and humor to set an emotional tone and intimate setting. Hillary Horan has the knack for choosing remembered events that few of us would have the courage to write about. She wrote "The Swollen Penis" because it was a particularly harrowing day for her terminally ill elderly father and she wanted to share the terror of taking care of someone who once was a giant figure in her life who has now become basically helpless. This has become a universal experience for most of us in this writing group, as I know it is for most of the middle-aged "sandwich generation."

Hillary describes taking her father to the hospital for a routine blood test and the reader is intimately involved every step of the way because of her writing style, which is casual and conversational, her authentic voice, not only in dialogue with her father but also with the nurses, both cranky and helpful whom she has come to know, and the doctors. She keeps her sanity as she waits for the results of her father's tests by phone calls home to her mother and daughter.

"Stretched nerves forbid me to read or watch television. I call my mother. 'Stuart is home,' she tells me. Thank God, they're not dead. I talk to my daughter. It is already dinner time and she has a test to study for at home. When Dad and I set out for the lab, we thought we would be home by mid-day. No one had any idea that the quick trip to draw blood would become a ten-hour stay. I hear my sweet little girl trying to comfort me as I fight to keep my anxiety from exploding through the phone at her."

Hillary's memoir is both poignant and humorous. She wanted her story to be funny because she feels that without humor, the task of caretaking one's parent is unbearable. "If you look hard enough, you can find a laugh," she reflects about this phase of her life. "Throughout this experience, I am an emotional reporter; I simply write down events and somehow attach my feelings to the piece. I find the intimacy that is ever evolving between my parents and myself very interesting and satisfying."

Hillary speaks of emotional reporting; one of the steps to writing a successful memoir is to go for the emotional truth of a situation and make the reader care not only for you, as narrator, but for the people in your life. The truth of Hillary's situation is that she was scared to death about what was happening to her father and when you have no control over losing someone so close to you, that level of terror then applies to everyone else in your life. She called home, not only to report why it was taking so long at the lab but also to find out if everyone else she loved was safe.

By the end of the piece, the reader cares about all of Hillary's family members because of the force of her language, the strength of her insight, the skill of her storytelling, and the fact that she reveals universal emotions we all share in the face of illness or death of an aging parent. Sometimes I hear a student say, "I'm not that important; why would anyone be interested in reading about my life?" The answer is that no life is insignificant and each one of us can find a piece of ourselves in another's memories. Memoirs such as Hillary's give us hope, inspiration, and the comfort to know that we are not alone in the world with our deep and insolvable human concerns.

I CALLED MY FATHER

VINCENT

By Bairbre Dowling

"This is my sleeping time," he roared sitting bolt upright in the mahogany marriage bed. It happened almost every time I forgot to get the hairbrush. The loudness in the darkened room, the furious tone, the edge to his voice stopping me in my creeping tracks, right under the gold framed picture of their marriage certificate signed by the Pope or some big Bishop in Rome.

"This is my sleeping time," the tone more wounded, stacatto, the level dropping slightly as it was now focused towards me. The lone maroon-uniformed figure, as yet, shoeless, hair disheveled. Projected towards me rather than to the whole thoughtless household beyond this curtained sanctuary.

"Sorry Vin," I whisper trying to return the bedroom to its predisturbed state. "I just need to get the hair brush." I inch my way toward the velvet—curtained bay window as he thumps his pillow in exasperation, huffing and puffing. I open the curtain just enough to slip my right hand in to feel around on the glass top on the bay window and grab the brush but even the muted

early morning light is harsh and white and just too much, the
final indignity.

"Aah—" the wounded bear growls at his ungrateful daughter.
Didn't she know he'd been out late, working all night? I run from
the room leaving the curtains parted and the light pouring into
the tomb, the bedroom door wide open. I take the stairs down two
at a time, arms out-stretched, one on the banister, one on the
wall still gripping the hair brush, landing heavily, with both feet
each time, to cover any other voiced rage that might be coming
from the pillaged bedroom. Quickly into the warm breakfast
kitchen, I shut the door.

"Mammy, can you brush my hair—I'll be late for the bus?"

"What's goin' on upstairs?"

"I had to get the hair-brush. I forgot to get it out last night."

"Was that the Boy Wonder I heard?" Mammy says feeding
the baby and salvaging the cindered toast from the grill. "He's
like a bear with a sore head," I say in the we-know-the-score-
club tone of voice. "Here let me do something to that hair of
yours," she says taking the brush, "before you miss the quarter
past eight."

*   *   *

Around the same time or before or after or whenever I was
still wearing little cotton dresses, I was caught off guard playing
with the boys in the back lane. We were bored walking walls and
robbin' apples n' rhubarb and annoying the heart out of the aul'
one on the corner of Shanowen Drive by climbing up on her
corrugated garage roof dancing and singing and jeering her until
someone had the brilliant idea we should show each other our
bottoms.

I must have gone first. My drawers were around my ankles
and my behind was in the air, all the fellas were gathered around,
at the very end of the lane and Vincent appeared and caught me
like that. I'd never seen him in our back lane before—ever. He

never called me in but this day he found me surrounded, exposed. A couple of gasps from the O'Carrolan boys warned me of disaster. "Hello Mr. Dowling," mumbled a couple from the Cinder Lane.

"Pull up your pants Barbara," he said in neutral tones, "And come home. Your Tea is ready."

He turned and disappeared from my view, returning down the lane.

"You're in for it now," my turncoat comrades hissed at me as I pulled myself together on the run. "You're in for it." I started crying as I climbed over the back gate.

As I ran up the path in the back garden the crying resounded in my whole body, a tinny sound and I felt how sad it was I might be leaving this world—that I had messed it up now—it would never be right. Vincent would never like me now. And I ran faster dreading my destination and hoping too, for an instant, he might be gone. He might have left for the Theater already and I could tell Mammy exactly what happened. She'd understand.

Vincent was there. We sat for hours on the second step of the stairs in the hall, looking at the hall table, the mirror, the glass front door—squashed beside each other on that narrow stairs. Nobody came to rescue me 'til bedtime. I just cried 'til every thing inside me swelled.

He told me all sorts of sensible things, I'm sure for my own protection, but all I remember is the shame, the mortification. He really spoiled my fun. There was no fun left in the world, only seriousness. I cried and cried and cried.

*   *   *

Around the same time or before, but during the time he lived with us, I was sent upstairs to get him up as he was going to be late for rehearsal at the Abbey. He had already been called twice and I was dispatched as a last resort. I knew from previous occasions it wouldn't be easy, so for a laugh I got a wet face cloth and an egg cup full of cold water.

Louise, my sister, came with me. We laughed when he shot up from prone to standing once the cold water touched his head. We just hadn't bargained for him being so disgusted with us. "Don't you know how hard I work, providing for you all, doing two jobs, writing radio scripts, and being a radio D.J. all morning and then rehearsing one show during the day and playing a different show at night? You must have been put up to this!" the outraged father tells his cruel girls.

But *I* knew. 'Cos Mammy already told me.

The curtain came down at half past ten, but it was common knowledge that after the pubs closed at eleven, if you were an actor and you tapped on the window of Groome's Hotel with a thruppence and waited for Patty Groome to peep at you through the curtains to let you in, or tell you to walk around the block 'til the Garda Siochana were definitely gone—you could get a drink there till two or three in the morning.

That's a long day and only five hours to go before the Hairbrush Invasion. No wonder Vincent was a bit cross.

THE WISDOM

OF SOLOMON

By Dorothy S. Huebel

He was bigger than the Colossus of Rhodes, braver than Sitting Bull, stronger than Sampson, better looking than Ramon Navarrro, and wiser than Solomon. And, he was my father—mine, mine alone. He was not really my brother's father. I was four years older than my brother, and I had a five year old's idea of what the "F'" word meant. After all, I grew up in farm country and no one could have convinced me that my parents would ever be involved in anything that icky. So I knew Donald had to have been adopted, and I, like Athena, had sprung from my father's head. I never really figured out how she got to be my mother, but as long as she cooked, cleaned and took care of us, I couldn't worry about the biological trifles, but then what five year old would?

He was perfect, a perfect father, a perfect citizen—member of the school board, President of the Chamber of Commerce, trustee of the Methodist Hospital, a 32nd degree Mason, an Elk, and the town's leading merchant. It didn't seem possible that I could ever find a single chink in my idol's armor, but it was there. You couldn't grow up in the 30's and not know the difference between Republicans and Democrats.

I never changed my affiliation nor did he. And, while I never loved him less for being so misguided, I questioned his judgment. Then George McGovern, my classmate, decided to run for public office in a state known as a Republican stronghold. George had no money, no name recognition, no political experience, and he was a Democrat.

We'd gone all through school together, he'd worked in my father's store, we'd been on the same debate team, and I endorsed his every stance, even though I'd have been hard pressed to articulate any one of them.

All he really needed was office space and there was an empty first floor office in one of my father's buildings, just as there were lots of empty spaces in every building in town since no one could afford to pay rent. Imagine how shocked yet impressed I was when I heard my father say, during one of my semi-annual visits home, that he had given that space to George saying, "It doesn't say much for democracy when an honorable, thinking man, even one with whom I don't agree, can't afford to run for office. And, I would like to think that in some small way I am righting that wrong."

Just before the Fourth of July George and his supporters painted the space, and moved in old desks, chairs and typewriters. Then they hung a big banner in the window announcing the opening of the George McGovern headquarters.

The next morning the officers of the Republican Women's Club marched down Main street in full regalia, which in those days meant hats and white gloves. They flew in the front door of my father's store like a covey of geese headed north and demanded an explanation.

"How could you, a member of the Republican State Committee, rent space to that man?" honked Mrs. Fredricks, the mayor's wife. "Yes, how could you do such a thing?" flapped her mother, the wife of the former mayor. The Fredricks had a dynastic lock hold on that office for years.

"Ladies, ladies, sit down and calm yourselves. Let me tell you the story behind the story, what really happened," he responded. "What you say is absolutely right, I did rent the space to George for $20 a month, July through November. What you don't know is that I am making a contribution to the Republican party in the full amount of the rent I will collect." And, with that he sat down and wrote out a check for one hundred dollars, one hundred dollars he had no intention of collecting.

He really was bigger than the Colossus of Rhodes, braver than Sitting Bull, stronger than Sampson, but best of all, my father was as wise, if not wiser, than Solomon.

THE SWOLLEN PENIS

By Hillary Horan

As I visit with my parents in their living room in Burbank, my eleven year old daughter, Rosie, plays quietly in the back of the house. The chit-chat is light, what Chinese food to order for dinner, where Rosie and I will sleep tonight during our private slumber party at Nonnie and Papa's. I turn the conversation to tomorrow's errands, one of the many conversations on this subject. My eighty-four-year-old father and eighty-one-year-old mother need a hand these days and it's my hand they get.

"So Dad, we'll head out to the lab at Kaiser tomorrow morning and get your blood taken and then I can run you guys wherever you need to go."

"You need to go see Dr. Nathan tomorrow," my mother tells me mysteriously. Dr. Nathan is Dad's oncologist.

"We do?" I look at my father. It seems that he no longer speaks the language.

"There's a new problem your father doesn't want to tell you about."

I go into diplomat mode. Something tells me I should have this information.

"Well, Dad, I'm sort of one of your main care-givers. It might be helpful for me to know if there's something new going on."

Silence, silence. He still can't speak English.

"His penis is swollen," my mother gently reveals.

I look at my father. "Are you sure?" He looks at me as if he can't believe my question.

"Yes, I'm sure."

"He just told me today. He said its been like that for three or four days and he just told me today." My mother, so clearly annoyed, much like she's been through the entire fifty-nine years of their marriage.

"Why didn't you say anything, Dad?" He is mute again.

"Were you hoping it would just go away?" He looks at me as if I have just provided him with a revelation.

"Yes."

The next morning I leave my mother and daughter at the house and take my father to Kaiser to have his blood drawn. It is raining. Not just a shower. I'm talking Bible story type pouring. The flat streets of the San Fernando Valley are already flooded. I work hard not to show my distress over how deep the water is at the hospital intersection. Visions of a stalled car crowd my head. My weakened father, his legs nearly non-operational. What the hell will I do if the car stalls out?

We reach the hospital and I wait to be able to drop him off in a covered area. Going to Kaiser is a whole different kind of adventure. Deep breathing is definitely required. I summon patience I never knew I had as I wait for a woman who looks a thousand years old get helped out of her wheelchair and into her car.

"Geez, Dad. Look at her. With all our problems we're still so lucky."

"You bet."

That's another thing I've learned to do beautifully. Lie. Find the silver lining in the dark clouds of lymphoma and chemotherapy.

After Dad gets his blood drawn, we make our way up to 301. Oncology. I hold his hand as we slowly walk down the hall. Everything hurts him. Every simple task is a monumental chore.

I feel as if I'm going to cry but I don't. I'll cry alone in the car. I'll cry on my bedroom floor after yoga. I'll cry with my husband in bed. I won't cry now.

We get to the desk in oncology.

"Hey, Robin." Of course, I know everyone.

"Hi, how are you today," the perky girl behind the desk in the death-ward chirps.

"Ah, not so good. Is it possible for Dad to see any of the oncologists? We don't care who, we don't care when. We like everybody."

"I don't know, I'll check. What's the problem?"

Man, she would have to ask that.

"Well, well," I stammer like an idiot. My father, looking again like he just arrived on Ellis Island, stares blankly. "Well, he's having some pain and swelling in his groin and . . . . male organ area." Good, got that one out. Never even had to say the word "penis."

"I'll see what I can do." The desk girl disappears. I hold no hope. Dropping in on your doctor at Kaiser is sort of like banging on the gates of Buckingham Palace declaring that you simply must have a moment with the Queen.

The desk girl reappears. "I'm sorry, they're booked solid. Go down to the appointment desk on the first floor and tell them you need to see an internist."

"All right, Robin. Thanks." We walk away from the cheery desk decorated with angels, paper hearts and teddy bears. Do they try to trick their ravaged patients by creating a happy environment?

"My father's oncologist wants him to see an internist today," I tell the bored woman at the appointment desk.

"What's the problem?" she asks, staring at her computer monitor. Geez, again with the probing question. At least I have my tidy little answer.

"He's experiencing some swelling around his male organ," I say expertly.

She gives us an appointment in the neighboring building.

"Dad, honey. I'll bring the car up to the overhang again and drive us over." The building we need is right next door, but even if it weren't raining, he could never make the walk. I run through the landslide of water and get to the car. When we get to the other building there is no overhang. I get out of the car with the sopping umbrella and walk him inside. I park, and once again, run through the relentless rain.

When we see Dr. Gruen, a doctor who is a stranger to us, I like him immediately. He wears a yarmulke and resembles a rabbi. His face is kind and he looks me right in the eye when I talk.

"Dr. Gruen," I hurriedly whisper while Dad is in the bathroom. "My father has lymphoma, he's in chemo right now, but we came today because out of nowhere, his penis is swollen. I don't want to be in the room when you examine him, because, well, yikes. He's just horrified that I have to be in on this latest development. But will you please get me as soon as you're done? He's not remembering anything anymore."

"Sure," he tells me. Dr. Gruen is adorable. I leave while he examines my father. I pace the hall until I am summoned into the room.

"I want to send him to emergency to have the fluid extracted from his abdomen." This is like when the mechanic tells you your water pump is about to go and if you don't have it replaced this minute you'll break down in the middle of the desert and die.

"All right."

"I'll get my nurse to do the paperwork," he vanishes.

"I don't want to have this done without Dr. Nathan knowing," my father says pitifully from the examining table.

I hate being the grown-up. It's bad enough to have to be the grown-up with my children, but now I have to do it with my parents. The cell phone in my purse rings. "Hello?"

"Hello, deah. What's going on?" My mother couldn't stand

the wait. She stares at the clock and wonders while Rosie eats all the food in her house.

"Has Stuart called?"

"No," she answers. This day just gets worse. Since I was spending the night in Burbank, my husband and our fifteen year old son, Gus, decided to run away on a male bonding overnight to Santa Barbara. I don't like Stuart's driving in ideal conditions and here he is covering a hundred miles of highway on a day that Noah could easily cruise down Wilshire.

"Man, I wish he'd call. But listen, the internist, Dr. Gruen, wants to extract the fluid from Dad's stomach over in emergency."

"I don't think you should do that. Dr. Nathan hasn't ordered that. See if you can contact Dr. Nathan and see what he says."

"Oh, Mom, I don't know. Getting a hold of the doctors around here is like trying to call the Pope. Dad has reservations, too. Let me quiz the doc and I'll call you back."

The nice rabbi doctor comes back. I pounce.

"Dr. Gruen, I need to ask you some questions. Everybody's freaked out about doing this procedure without the go-ahead from Dr. Nathan." Dr. Gruen looks at me and says that this won't interfere with the chemo, it won't aggravate the lymphoma and that it's common practice for this type of cancer patient.

"It will only make him more comfortable," Dr. Gruen explains. "If it were my father, I would go ahead with the extraction."

"Yeah, but do you like your father?" I ask.

"I love my father." I believe this doctor. We prepare to face the rain and go to emergency.

When we reach emergency, a nice nurse checks us in while Tess, the cranky nurse, tells me to leave. She will not hand over any information, like how long this is going to take for instance. Stretched nerves forbid me to read or watch television. I call my mother.

"Stuart is home," she tells me. Thank God, they're not dead. I talk to my daughter. It is already dinner time and she has a test to study for at home. When Dad and I set out for the lab, we thought we would be home by mid-day. No one had any idea that the quick trip to draw blood would become a ten-hour stay. I hear my sweet little girl trying to comfort me as I fight to keep my anxiety from exploding through the phone at her.

"It's all right, Mommy. Do what you have to do and I'll be fine."

She's so good to me. I get off the phone as options fly through my head. What if he has to stay in the hospital overnight? Isn't shoving a needle in someone's gut and taking garbage out sort of a big deal? How can he go home? I can't leave my mother alone. What if she has one of her nosebleeds or a low blood-sugar attack. I'm about to jump out of my skin when I remember I have a brother who is willing, able and pretty close by. Maybe I should call Brian and have him come by the hospital. He can take Dad home, he can sleep at Mom's if Dad can't come home, I can get Rosie home, I can jump off a bridge. The rain is showing no mercy. The freeway will be a disaster. Breathe, breathe, breathe.

I see Tess, the mean nurse, wheel out a man who looks much older and more frail than my father. I need information, so I pretend to be confused.

"Tess, is that my father?"

"No, but he is done. You can go back now."

I fly through the double doors of emergency and start poking my head in doorways to find my father. There he is, in the last room, lying on a bed.

"Hey, hon," I say to my Dad. "How you holding up in here?"

He points to five, one litre bottles. They are full of what looks like thin buttermilk.

"This is what they took out of me," he says in astonishment.

"Gross, really? My God, there's five of them."

"The doctor says its the equivalent of ten pounds."

"Oh, man. Unbelievable. Do you feel better?"

"Yes. I feel remarkably better. It's amazing. Look at all of that."

The doctor comes in. He looks like he's nine years old.

"Doctor, what is that stuff?" I ask.

"It's fluid and lymphoma. This isn't a permanent solution, the lymphoma secretes fluid, but he should feel relieved for a couple of weeks."

"Are there instructions on how I should care for him, I mean regarding this procedure?"

"Just keep the puncture clean. It's small. The chance of infection is unlikely." He sails out. I turn to my father to help him get his shirt on. Like everything else, dressing has become difficult for him, too.

"Geez, Dad, this is great. I'm so happy we decided to do this."

"Me, too."

"You're such a typical man, Dad. Won't complain about anything until something's wrong with your dick."

He stares into space, back on Ellis Island. There is some territory I can't enter with my father. It seems so silly to me. He's a man, doesn't every man have a penis? Doesn't he realize I have a husband and a son? That's two close relatives who own a penis. Poor baby, so self-conscious of this organ. The tunnel from which I flew to begin my journey through life.

"Let's beat it, Dad. I've got a high strung filly at home who needs to study for a grammar test." Slowly and happily, we make our way to the front of emergency. The rain has stopped and I walk under the dark blue sky that is impossibly clear. As I get the car and drive to my father I feel thankful for the closure on this day. I'm afraid it will be one of the last with a happy ending.

CHAPTER FIVE

Children

Readers often look for memoirs about raising children not only for guidance about how to understand their child's developmental issues, but also for companionship in the complex job of child rearing, a job few of us have been trained to do. All of the writers in this anthology are mothers; some are grandmothers, some have been single mothers, some are stepmothers. We've seen it all and done it all, had the same joys and shed the same tears and made the same mistakes every other parent makes raising children whether today or yesterday.

The pleasures and woes of being a parent are universal. Unfortunately, there are few memoirs written about the parent-child relationship from the parent's perspective, probably because there is no time to write when one is fully immersed in the job of parenting and may also have a part or full-time job outside the home. So most of us have to wait until the little darlings, as well as ourselves, are older. Anne Lamott's *Operation Instructions* about the first year of her son's life and *Traveling Mercies* which details their life together when he is nine are exceptions.

Jacqueline Connolly begins this section with a very poignant piece about how a memory from her own childhood foretells a living reality in her adult life. As a young child, Jackie witnessed a red-haired mailman having an epileptic seizure on the sidewalk near her suburban house. She was fascinated with the event, as a six-year-old might be, but she had a premonition even then that she would experience this event again sometime in the future.

She was reminded of this "Imprint" when her eleven-year-old red-haired son started having seizures as a result of a surgical trauma to his brain. Jackie is our in-house philosopher; she makes us think about the effect of powerful memories on our lives. She asks: "Are certain events, certain memories meant as mystical forewarnings, fleeting moments when all the tenses of our lives—past, present, future—merge together in one transcendental whole?"

The essence of memoir is to track the writer's thoughts

struggling to achieve some understanding of a problem. Memoirists are adept at letting the reader in on their personal queries. They ask the questions we all wish we thought to ask.

What one doesn't understand is as good a place to start investigating the mysteries of one's life as exploring the things we do know and understand. There is always more to find out. Jackie asks us to look at our past memories as clues to our present or future realities. She reminds us of St. Augustine who wrote in his *Confessions*: "The present time of things past is memory; the present time of things present is sight; the present time of things future is expectation." A well-written memoir makes us think about how memory helps shape a life.

Hillary Horan wrote "Miss Rose Kathleen" as an ode to her eleven-year-old daughter, Rosie. Hillary is the youngest member of our merry band of memoirists, a full-time mother with a pre-adolescent daughter and an adolescent son. She writes about her own feelings of inadequacy as a parent raising a dynamic daughter whom she adores, but who utterly confuses her. She reminds us of the universal experience we all have as parents as our "baby" reaches the threshold to adolescence. We want to keep our youngsters children to avoid the battles we know will ensue as they make their way to independence. Hillary reflects:

"Writing about Rosie helps me embrace the issues that arise raising a daughter. As she enters the eternally baffling stage of young womanhood, I have to forever be on my toes." Hillary also writes about her children to avoid slipping into the safe world of denial in which she was raised in the sixties. She knows the world holds many more challenges for our children than it presented to our parents thirty years ago. That's what keeps her alert.

Hillary wrote this memoir in the form of a poem in the second person narrative, to muse upon her innermost thoughts about her daughter and to reflect on the courage she, herself, will need as Rosie moves into womanhood.

"I will have courage
I will not deny or turn away.
Ride the biggest wave in the ocean
I fly into the mouth of the dragon."

My own piece, "Christmas Tree Light Psychosis" is written to my young son who is now a man in his early thirties. This short memoir recalls a time when I was a newly divorced single mother facing Christmas alone with my children, obsessed with an irrational need to decorate the Christmas tree perfectly. When I read this piece aloud at readings, I know from the moans of recognition I hear that this is not particular to me! In the piece, my son Brendan decides to take over the task of stringing the Christmas tree lights which, upon reflection, is an offer that could be seen as both foolhardy and courageous.

"Mom, I'd like to do the lights this year.

Are you sure? You know what that means?

Yes, I know you want them just right and I can do them.

Why don't you go upstairs and Heather and I will call you when we're done?"

I use humor and tension in this piece because of my own embarrassment about being so neurotic about the perfect placement of Christmas tree lights and ornaments, a trait I inherited from my father. One of the elements of memoir is to be an authentic narrator; to be willing to expose your foibles and distortions and laugh at yourself. The trick is to remember that you, yourself are not that important, except insofar as your example can shine a light on a universal human trait and help the reader feel a little less bizarre himself!

I wish I could say that I get a kind of Martha Stewart thrill out of feverishly decorating the Christmas tree; unfortunately, the feeling that arises for me is closer to Robert DiNiro's anxiety in "Analyze This." The ingenuity of my young son's solution to the Christmas tree light dilemma entertained me thoroughly and somehow its absurdity broke the spell of my perfectionism. I hope it works for you too!

Ruth Bracken writes about a very important transition in the life of mother and child—when her child moves out. In "Moving In," Ruth is about to move into a house she has bought twelve miles away from the rental where she has raised her son as a single mom. Her eighteen-year-old son decides not to come with her. As Ruth packs boxes for the move, she describes her feelings of loss through her internal dialogue and the reader is invited to take an intimate look at her relationship with her son:

"Who will make coat hanger toys to drive the kitties wild? Who else would ask me to get a tattoo? Who else would name a solid black cat 'Ice?'

Who will say 'I love you, Mom' in a husky voice just before bed? And what will I miss first? Your eyes: the open color of possibilities."

Ruth is skilled at weaving realities; she turns articles of her son's clothing and discarded toys into tales of their life together. In the process, she also recalls the time when she left home when she and her divorced mother parted on the curb in front of New York University. Ruth expresses a universal emotional truth about parental love and the passing of time we can all understand:

"It's so ironic, I moan to a good friend. Children come into our lives, and just when you've gotten completely used to them and their lives are indispensable to you, they leave you behind, staring at the dirty walls."

IMPRINTS

By Jacqueline Connolly

It's funny, sometimes disturbing, the things we remember from childhood. Looking back on the events of my life, I wonder if those small, specific memories that cling, little incidents apart from one's daily routine, are not meant as warnings—forewarnings of the future. Perhaps something happens that makes one think: wait a minute, I've been here before. What was it? Oh, yes, that time when I was a child—*now* I know why I could never forget that scene.

Is this why I remember so clearly those two times I witnessed epileptic seizures? Were they meant as premonitions? "Remember this because we will come back—take note, prepare yourself."

The first time it happened I could not have been more than six or seven. My mother, sister and I were crossing a side street in Glendale on our way to visit my grandmother; we had almost reached the curb when I sensed a commotion behind me and then heard a strange, loud, moaning. I turned and saw a red-haired man dressed in a blue mailman's uniform lying on the street between the white lines of the pedestrian lane. His prone body was jerking around in wild motions. Next to him, a brown leather mail bag lay askew with the letters that had fallen out scattered on the pavement.

I asked my mother what was wrong with him but she just kept trying to hurry me along, offering some vague explanation; she probably said he was having a "fit" as that was the term commonly used then. But I didn't want to move on, I was worried about this man, wondering if anyone from the crowd that had gathered around could help him. I still see him clearly, all the colors highlighted by the brightness of the sun as it centered on this blue-clad figure with his bright orange hair, convulsing on the dark asphalt.

Then when I was fourteen, I was having a snack at the drugstore counter in Hollywood with a few school friends. Suddenly, I became aware of strange sounds and movements emanating from the young man sitting next to me. Something was wrong, I knew, so picking up my plate, glass and school books, I found an empty seat on the other side of the U shaped counter, an unplanned vantage point from which to watch the drama taking place before me. I now realized that the young man was having a seizure. A woman sitting on the other side of the man was holding his body in her arms, trying to protect him, trying to still the spasms. Somehow I knew she was his mother—a rather gaunt woman wearing a black coat, her mottled gray hair pulled back in a knot. I can't remember what he looked like, only the woman holding him to her and the sad, worried expression on her face. I had recently seen the movie, "Grapes of Wrath," and it was easy to imagine that these two figures had somehow evolved from that stark setting.

Why, I wondered, was he making those strange, frightening sounds, blowing bubbles of saliva out of his mouth? Then, becoming aware of others around the woman trying to help, I thought should I have stayed in my seat? Guilt surged through me—what should I have done? Did people think I was reacting as if he were a leper or something? Yet wouldn't I have been in the way if I had stayed? Where were my friends, had they moved, too? I didn't search for them; I was mesmerized by the scene taking place in front of me, the fusing together of these two desolate forms.

It was not until he was eleven years old that my son, my red-haired son, started having seizures as a result of surgical trauma to his brain. Fortunately, medication was able to control them until he reached adulthood. Now it is he who suffers seizures in restaurants—in restaurants, buses, on streets, at work, in the gym. Since he lives apart from us, I am frequently not with him and feel sad to think that often all he sees are the faces of strangers when consciousness returns.

Yet I have been that woman. I have cradled my son's body in my arms, shielding his head before gently lowering him onto the floor while waiting for the spasms to ease, the guttural moans subside, wiping away the saliva as it gurgles from his mouth. The fallen mailman, the protective mother, were they there to lead the way, to reassure me, to say, "You are not alone; this, too, can be endured?"

I am not a fatalist. I do not believe our lives are predetermined, neither can I believe that the effect of these powerful memories on my life are mere coincidence. Are certain events, certain memories meant as mystical forewarnings, fleeting moments when all the tenses of our lives—past, present, future— merge together in one transcendental whole?

MOVING IN

By Ruth Bracken

Today—I am alone with an overdose of melancholy, mixed with memories and spring rain. A downpour is rare in our parched irrigated-desert city, and I am grateful for the camouflage. It matches my tears. Downstairs, ten packed boxes and many more unsealed cardboard containers line up haphazardly against the bare blue walls. Tape, scissors and piles of bubble wrap lie scattered on the floor. Neither you nor I really lives here anymore; it's the chaos of the half-packed.

Today is also the day before your eighteenth birthday, and I don't know where you are. It's Easter break and you are out and about. You might be working, registering for junior college, looking for an apartment, getting ready for a surfing trip to Mexico, hanging out with your best friend, James, talking on the phone to Elena or Ashley—any combination of the above.

Eighteen years ago on this day I knew exactly where you were, though we had not yet officially met. Monday, April 20, 1982 began with a crackling hot morning coated with smog. I remember the relief of the hospital's air conditioning exhaling chilly air on my bare arms and round belly when I first checked in. Thirty-six hours later, give or take a medical procedure or two, you pushed your valiant way out. And after I held you, nothing was ever the same again.

You have chosen not to come with me to the house I have bought. It is a humble stucco box, due east of Venice on the quieter edges of Hollywood. Twelve miles by the path of a determined crow who doesn't have to use the freeway. In three weeks, I will be moving there without you; you'll be staying with your Dad until you find an apartment. Moving miles away from the beach doesn't work for you; staying on the Westside no longer fits me. It's time for a change, for both of us. We are parting, the kind of natural separation one prepares oneself for endlessly and insufficiently.

"It's so ironic," I moan to a good friend. "Children come into our lives, and just when you've gotten completely used to them and their lives are indispensable to you, they leave you behind, staring at the dirty walls."

While packing up a box of photographs, I recall my own mother and my last long summer at home, before I flew away to New York. Our final journey together was very quiet. On Fifth Avenue, my mother and I studied the subway maps, stared upward at the skyscrapers and shopped silently for my winter wardrobe. On the last day of September, my mother left me without a word, standing alone on the curb of New York University, autumn leaves turning orange and falling down all around me. Years later she told me how many of those miniature bottles of airplane liquor she consumed on her flight back home alone. She who rarely drank at all.

I do not drink much either, and cannot find an appropriate container to hold my pain. Last week, as I packed in the living room, you started in on your room. Tossing out T-shirts you hadn't worn for five years, sweaters that never fit, bright red Lego cranes, covered with dust and spaceships with blue men trapped inside. Your magazines, months and years of "Surfer" and "Surfing" were packed carefully into their own special boxes, the ones you'll be taking with you.

I glanced over at you, walking through the living room carrying the first of the boxes. I wanted to ask you impossible questions. Who now will whistle brightly in the early morning?

Who will make coat hanger toys to drive the kitties wild? Who else would ask me to get a tattoo? Who else would name a solid black cat "Ice;" who else will say "I love you, Mom," in a husky voice, just before bed? And what will I miss first? Your eyes: the open color of possibilities.

Pieces of you will come with me, of course. The double-handed vase you made for my last birthday, pictures of you at nine months, then snapshots at eight years old, blowing bubbles in the backyard. Your smoothly produced graduation smile. You said you thought you looked like a used-car salesman; your godmother swore you resembled her stockbroker. I'll carefully pack every present you've given me: the silver engraved jewelry box, the teddy bear sitting in his white wicker chair, your first ink drawing of waves. Those things, and a thousand unboxed memories.

After my first year at New York University, I returned home for the summer to find that my mother had moved from the home in the hills where I had grown up. Divorced and living alone, she had faced the task of packing up her memories, her children's leftovers and her miserable years with my father.

My mother's new house was small and Spanish, hidden behind rangy shrubs on a shady street in West Los Angeles. A huge avocado tree spread its arms over most of the backyard. Although I never lived there, I visited enough to grow used to it. A few years later I was married under that tree, a mad squirrel throwing avocados down on the small crowd.

Perhaps there is no other way through this foggy ache of separation, except one damp step at a time. My mother started her life anew, and so will I. As soon as I have all these memories boxed and sealed.

*   *   *

Postscript: one month later

This is my house now. I walk through the rooms, followed sometimes by either Ice or Sam. I'm learning the cracks in the floor, the oddities of old electrical outlets, the heat of different rooms, where to stand for the best evening breeze. Whose dogs bark in the evening, whose cats challenge mine after midnight. Trying to memorize my neighbor's names. Laying out the design for the garden, using discarded bricks and pieces of rock the former owners left behind. Waking before dawn to trace the patterns of eastern light on my bedroom walls.

Learning to get through the morning without your whistle, without remembering what I miss. Coming through April and out into May, learning to move in with myself.

MISS ROSE KATHLEEN

By Hillary Horan

You are eleven years old now.
My youngest child
My girl.

I love to sleep with you.
Last night Daddy announced
"I've got this rotten cold, I'll sleep in the guest room,
Otherwise I'll keep you up all night."
We smile at each other
A happy conspiracy.

What luck, we say
Snuggling into flannel sheets.
"My sweet little baby," I stroke your impossibly soft cheek.
"My sweet little mama," you playfully mock.

In the morning you cry.
A math test
Dreaded, hateful math.
You are afraid, brimming with anxiety.
Positive you will forget everything you already know.

Why do you beat yourself up?
Can't you see you have it all.
The world will continue to spin
Even if you make mistakes.
Sometimes I don't know how to be your mother.
I encourage you to relax, don't care so much
I am accused of being unsupportive.
I tell you not to worry, you will ace it.
You say I am putting pressure on you.

I swear I have no expectations
But with your good looks and fine humor
can't you just have fun?
Marry well and be the incredible mother that you will be.

I apologize.
I am politically incorrect.
Of course, you knew that already.

Time for bed.
Tonight you sleep alone.
Before dreams, cartwheels.

I sit in bed, a magazine on my lap
Looking at pictures of women who are younger and thinner than
     me.
The corner of my eye
Catches you in flight.

Over and upside down you go
Your legs and arms the spokes of the spinning wheel you imitate.
You look perfect to me.

"Rosie," I plead
"It's too late for this, calm down. You'll hurt your wrists."
"Just one more," you gasp.
Just ten more.

I tell you the stories of teenage daughters and mothers
Fighting
Homes become battlefields.
Both struggling to accept the inevitable transformation.

"That will never happen to us," you say impatiently.
At this point, inconceivable to you.
I am afraid
I know the truth.

A young female,
Titanic emotions
Feelings allowed, encouraged.
They run fast and wild, a mad gazelle.

God help the man who falls in love with you
He'd best be tough.
He's best be the most wonderful man of his generation.

I will have courage
I will not deny or turn away
Ride the biggest wave in the ocean
I fly into the mouth of the dragon.

CHRISTMAS TREE LIGHT

PSYCHOSIS:

TO MY YOUNG SON

By Maureen Murdock

You know I've always had a slight seasonal psychosis that starts to develop in early December, grows in intensity as we go out to buy the Christmas tree and flourishes into full blossom the moment we take the Christmas tree lights out of the basement. I know I don't need to remind you; that's probably why you've always dreaded the holidays. And stay away.

It all started when I was a young girl in suburban New Jersey and my dad, your pop, dressed every outside fir tree, every rope of hanging evergreen inside and outside the house and of course, his piece de resistance, the Christmas tree with perfectly spaced, perfectly synchronized Christmas tree lights.

In the 50's there were the thick opaque colored bulbs of repeating sequences of blue, orange, yellow, green, red, and white each of which he replaced as soon as one burned out. We always had bulbs in reserve. The sixties brought the clear glass bulbs of the same colors that seemed to need fewer replacements. The seventies ushered in tiny clear glass bulbs that danced magically as pinpricks of white starlight when lit. Each bulb knew its place, its string hidden well by tree needles. Dad never allowed the cord that powered and held the lights together to show.

Each string was carefully arranged and attached to tree limbs so that the lights could peak out of the fullness of the tree's foliage. That's why it became important to buy just the right tree. And that's when I always started getting nervous.

When I was a child, going out to find just the right tree was fun but when I became a mother, it became a heartache. First of all, there was no snow to brush off the trees in Los Angeles and the trees seemed smaller, drier, more spindly and droopier than the trees I was used to on the East Coast. Secondly, the strong Douglas firs that I coveted for their ability to wear my carefully picked ornaments and lights with dignity were out of my price range. Each year's attempt to duplicate my memories of childhood magic became more painful as first, your dad and I, or later on, you and I failed to arrange the Christmas tree lights just right.

I know I must have made you and Heather miserable. My behavior warranted a preliminary DSM IV diagnosis. In fact, I think you were the one who said, "Mom, you have Christmas tree light psychosis," which you then tried to cure.

When you were nine, or maybe eleven, but not ten, I'm sure of that, we walked down the street to the small Boys' Club tree lot on Main and picked out a California spindly needle Christmas tree that we could carry back home. It was about five feet tall. When we got home you and Heather and I moved the couch out of the way and situated the tree in the annual tree corner near the front window of the living room. I started to sweat, get dry mouth, and the hair on the back of my neck started to rise. You looked at me and said:

"Mom, I'd like to do the lights this year."

"Are you sure? You know what that means?"

"Yes, I know you want them just right and I can do it."

"Why don't you go upstairs and Heather and I will call you when we're done."

So I went upstairs. And tried to sit still. I paced from my bedroom to the bathroom and back again to the bedroom. I laid down on my bed, looked up at the ceiling and I tried to breathe deeply. I considered the courage your request took. I wondered if you and Heather had planned this in private to alleviate another Christmas tree light drama or if yours had been a spontaneous gesture. I made a pact with myself that however the tree looked would be acceptable.

It was Heather's voice that called me downstairs. It seemed a little too soon to my mind for you to have done a careful job. But I had made a pact with myself so I quieted my critic and gingerly walked the stairs.

The tree was lit and it had a rackish tilt. It was clear that the lights were a-tangle. The colored lights (from the sixties) bunched up on the right side at the top of the tree and the white twinkle lights (from the seventies) drooped around the bottom. The glass balls were spaced more evenly.

"How do you like it mom?" said Heather. "I did the balls and Brendan did the lights."

"Yeah, I tried to give them a new look; I decided they wanted to be a bit freer this year. So I picked up the colored ones and threw them up over the top of the tree and where they landed they stayed. Looks pretty cool, doesn't it?"

I started to laugh. It did look cool. The tree looked happy— it looked like a well-licked ice cream cone that had started to melt. It was so incongruous to my obsessive light stringing nature that it tickled me completely. I laughed so hard I started to cry. And all of a sudden, years of trying to imitate my father's perfection washed away and my psychosis was cured. At least temporarily!

It is true that I have never had the wild abandon you displayed that day two decades ago to throw the lights up on the tree and let them fall where they may but some day, I hope I will.

CHAPTER SIX

Marriage

The writers in this section look at marriage after the first bloom of love and passion has fallen from the vine and the day-to-day realities of living with a mate one has chosen for better or for worse have settled in. The themes explored are varied, yet universal: travel, compromise, fidelity, and longing. Dorothy Huebel writes about the river boat trip she and her husband, Jack, took on the beautiful Blue Danube. Now, that sounds very romantic, doesn't it? The trip of a lifetime? However, Jack forgot to pack a very important piece of clothing and Dorothy describes the trip from a shopper's point of view, looking for men's underwear for 13 days in seven countries! In "Leave It to Beaver," Dorothy writes with her usual charm and attention to detail:

"If one is fortunate enough to first see Budapest from the deck of a river boat on the Danube as it glides beneath the Chain Bridge just as night falls, one is blessed with an indelible memory of incredible splendor—it's as if a necklace of lights had been strung on fairy tale castles mirrored in the oil slick flow of the Danube. I'll always remember that magic moment. My mate, on the other hand, missed it—he was sudsing his undies."

As I have written before, Dorothy's humor, a key element of memoir writing, keeps everyone in the group coming back to hear the next installment of her seventy-something year life. The energy of the group is important to each writer and one of the benefits of writing in a group is that each writer can identify her own writing weaknesses, as well as her strengths, by listening to the strengths of others. Dorothy says, "There is no one better at dialogue than Hillary and I know that is only one aspect of my writing which needs improvement. I revel in Janet's descriptive power and Marilyn's ability to string together words which reflect her soul." As you can tell from Dorothy's reflection, constructive comments and support are core aspects to a successful writing group.

The members of this writing group do not know each other's husbands. Some brave souls have come to our readings but several spouses have not. The only way we know the character of each other's spouse or ex-spouse is through our memoirs. In "My Peace with the Smoker," Marilyn Kierscey describes a territorial dispute between her and her husband about where he put his meat smoker in her garden in the backyard.

"Coming home Sunday, I found Ted in the back yard busily digging out plants. 'My English garden,' I screamed .... 'I thought they were weeds,' he said."

Marilyn's piece demonstrates the universality of different emotional sensitivities within a marriage and how, in a successful long-term marriage, husband and wife have to learn to respect each other's needs and compromise. Probably no one else in the group could have written about this incident with so little rancor. Dorothy is correct when she acknowledges Marilyn's ability to write in such a way that reflects her soul.

Hillary Horan uses dialogue like a pro. "The Trust Thing" takes place in a Thai restaurant in Palm Springs where she and her husband, Stu, talk around subjects such as weight loss, alcohol, sexuality, getting a job, and fidelity over kung pao chicken and curried green beans. Hillary always tackles touchy subjects with an edge of hilarity and compassion. She invites the reader into her reflections about trust and personal differences as we read the conversation she has with her husband.

"I'm afraid I'll have an affair." Well, that was good. Of all the people to tell.

"Why do you think that?" He doesn't look freaked out. His voice sounds relaxed.

"Because my ego is weak. I still want men to find me desirable."

After all these years of being happily married, I'm still pathetically weak.

There I said it. I'm just a whore. A sickening whore.

"You underestimate yourself. People who have affairs put out a vibe. You don't put out a vibe."

Stu never even put his chopsticks down. He's so
secure. What happened to him? I stare across the table.
If he just told me that he was afraid to do something out
in the world because he would be tempted to have an
affair, I'd probably have thrown the curried green beans
in his face and run sobbing out of the restaurant.

The immediacy and honesty in Hillary's writing helps the
reader explore the universality of communicating about a difficult
issue, such as fidelity, in a marriage. Hillary wanted to show that
married partners can successfully communicate rather than
fighting or freezing each other out. She wanted to explore the
fact that although she might have misgivings about trusting herself,
her husband does not.

At first, most memoirists do not know either the theme of
their memoir or their purpose in writing it. That often comes later;
after the piece has been written and rewritten. Hillary has endless
faith in her marriage partner's ability to share her life and have
healthy communication; that's why she wrote it.

In writing this piece, Hillary also brought up an issue that
many memoirists face. "How can I write about living people
without invading their privacy or hurting their feelings?" I always
advise my students to avoid anything that could bring harm in
any way to the principal they are writing about. A memoir is
always about the writer first, but we all have supporting characters
in our lives with whom we are intimately involved.

Writers deal with the issue of writing about living people in a
variety of ways. Some, like Hillary, show their writing to the person
named in the piece and discuss with them their feelings about
using the piece for publication. Others ask the other person to
read the piece and suggest changes if they are necessary. The
writer can then decide to make the change or not based on
whether the change would violate the emotional honesty of the
memoir. Some memoirists wait until the principals are dead; others
change names and identifying characteristics.

It is difficult, if not impossible, to change the name and identifying characteristics of a spouse without writing fiction, so Hillary waited several years before she felt comfortable enough with her writing and her motivation before she approached this very private part of her life.

In the next piece in this section, "Ours," Janet Smith writes about her dead husband with such love and sensitivity that she brings him back to life for the reader. Janet is our resident poet. As a memoirist she incorporates all of her senses in her writing and creates an atmosphere of place and emotion. In "Ours," Janet writes about the loss of her husband after fifty years of marriage. Janet had been a dancer and her writing reflects the sensuality that has always been part of her nature. When she sits down to write, she immerses herself in the sensations and images that shimmer throughout her body and imagination. She looks for the universality that ties her memory to the recollected experiences of others. "Ours" is a soulful attempt to retrieve the beauty of nature and her longing for her husband, as well as an acknowledgement of the poignant sense of abandonment that accompanies her new identity as a widow.

LEAVE IT TO BEAVER

By Dorothy S. Huebel

Take it from me, those who leave it to Beaver will end up with a dam and a pool of stagnating spontaneity, romance, and compassion lost. I know, because Beaver is my husband of many years. There was a time when I called that compulsive sports-fan, car-nut, clothes-buff "Honey, Dear or just Jack." Those endearments ended, however, when we took a ten day river boat trip on the beautiful Blue Danube with four additional days in Turkey. Silly me, I left it to Beaver and spent thirteen days in seven countries looking for men's underwear.

I can pack in a trice, a word like trice provides for greater flexibility than time specific. He needs three days and an outline. I have no objections to outlines, but I question a need for Arabic numbers, under the capital letters beneath the Roman numerals for listing the contents of two suitcases and a carry-on: I, II and III respectively. Suitcase I-A trousers, I-B shirts, a-dress, b-sports, I-C sweaters and I-D shoes, each shoe with it's wooden tree in it's own flannel bag. Color, where appropriate, indicated by lower case letters: a-black, b-brown, c-white. Five pairs of shoes for two weeks?

In suitcase II he packed jackets, underwear, pajamas, socks

and belts. Only he knew what was in III, besides a shaving kit, copies of Sports Illustrated and a jar of peanut butter. Yes, peanut butter. My husband's a fussy eater. I thought mankind learned long ago that tis folly to put all your underwear in one basket, so to speak.

We arrived in Vienna at noon. Vienna, the dream of a life time come true and we were actually in a cab waiting for the driver to retrieve our luggage, take us to the boat and then back to the city for an afternoon "at leisure". My luggage and Suitcase I were in Vienna. Suitcase II was "in transit." Hours and interminable forms later, a baggage supervisor authorized the purchase of necessities and gave us obsequious assurance that Suitcase II would catch up with us. "No Mien Herr, jackets are not a necessity, underwear is."

We were in the magical city of Vienna to buy men's underwear—no leisurely stroll on the Ringstrasse, no Sachertorte, and no Strauss concert in the park. We had a mission. We soon found that window-shopping in Vienna was not how one went about finding an establishment that sold what he was looking for. "Shpreken sie English?"—boxer shorts? briefs? tee shirts? "Nein." The key to the question was knowledge of the words *unter hosen* and *unter hemden*. I am convinced that Austrians know how to make art, music and culture but not undergarments. So, he spent $ 58.00 at a men's haberdashery in the Ring for the only pair of gros, batiste *unter hosen and unter hemden* made in Switzerland. We returned to the boat just in time to sail for the romantic old city of Bratislava, Czechoslovakia where there are no stores, ergo, no underwear nor anything else for sale.

If one is fortunate enough to first see Budapest from the deck of a river boat on the Danube as it glides beneath the Chain Bridge just as night falls, one is blessed with an indelible memory of incredible splendor—it's as if a necklace of lights had been strung on fairy tale castles mirrored in the oil slick flow of the Danube. I'll always remember that magic moment. My mate, on the other hand, missed it—he was sudsing his undies.

Hungarian is a language unlike any other modern language, therefore, underwear, *unter hosen, unter* or *ober* anything cuts no ice in Hungarian. So, as we strolled through the old city of Pest and the bustling metropolis of Buda, I grudgingly hoped he'd be lucky enough to see what he wanted on display. It was as if I were traveling alone; enjoying gypsy violins, savoring goulash and strudel, all the sights, smells and colors of the grandeur that was Budapest. I was as one with the Hapsburgs, treading the cobblestones of history, while the Beaver's eyes darted back and forth oblivious to all but what he sought.

Then we were in Belgrade with a choice of visiting Tito's Lodge or a trip to the new shopping mall. Out of deference to my spouse, I chose the latter—a grim, grey cement fortress, a monument to planned obsolescence built around a promenade with six spindly trees held captive by benches screwed to cement blocks, which in turn, were surrounded by jean-clad teen-agers slurping cokes. Where there are teen-agers and cokes, my husband reasoned, there had to be some kids who were learning English so he asked. "Yes," several answered and I think what they then said was "Good morning, this is a seat, that is a tree and my dog's name is Milosovic."

I stared in horror as the Beaver unbuckled his belt, pulled his shirt tails out of his pants, unbuttoned and took off his shirt and pointing to his Austrian *unter hemden* and the waist band of the *unter hosen*, he acted out the rest. It was magic. The Charade Master followed his entourage to a dark, dingy, windowless store for men. Minutes later, he emerged with two skimpy, ribbed undershirts and two pair of knee length boxer shorts made of starched cheese cloth—all four pieces costing the equivalent of $4.00. Now he was an investor averaging his costs.

He had no luck in Romania or Bulgaria. We arrived in Romania on a Sunday when everything was closed and in Bulgaria on a national holiday. But, it was there, at the mouth of the Danube, that we boarded a ship, not a boat, to sail down the Bosporus and into the heart of exotic Istanbul.

We had three days of vacation left, he had five sets of underwear, and we were in a hotel with over-night laundry service. I begged, I pleaded with him to forget his quest. But not the Beaver. Oh no, here in the city of minarets and mosques, astride Europe and Asia, he prowled the souks of the Great Bazaar looking for jockey shorts as I bought leather wallets, belts and silk scarves. Two days to go and my hopes of reveling in the arcane world of Constantinople were slipping from my grasp. I turned from the hotel window, put down the guide book, looked him straight in the eyes and said, as if I had just read a bit of historic trivia, "You know, you'll never find what you're looking for in Turkey. The Turks haven't worn undergarments since before the days of turbans and pantaloons. It was a practice instituted as an energy conservation measure for men with harems. Just another example of Turkish ingenuity." And, he believed me.

Suitcase II never left LAX, but a message on our answering machine told us to call and it would be delivered to our door. Marital harmony restored, I can now say, with just a tinge of rancor, that Jack is the only man I know who returned from a two week vacation with a suitcase full of clean clothes and I, the owner of Austrian/Swiss/Yugoslavian dust cloths, and a handful of gifts.

MY PEACE

WITH THE SMOKER

By Marilyn Kierscey

Several years ago, I heard the sounds of a huge truck stopping in front of our house. The driver pounded on our door. When I answered it, he didn't waste words. "Lady," he said, "This belongs in a restaurant."

"What are you talking about?" I asked impatiently. I was late for work and wanted him to leave.

"Come see for yourself," he said. He pulled the back of his truck open. Something that resembled a train engine was the only thing inside. It had a shiny stack about 12 feet high and a body about 8 feet long. Peering into the dark interior of the truck, I could see two wheels. For a second, I thought Ted had bought a train engine like the one Walt Disney had kept in his back yard. We have a small house and yard, and I couldn't understand where he thought he'd put it.

"It's a smoker for a restaurant, an INDUSTRIAL smoker," the driver said, "all the way from Smoky Joe's in Oklahoma. You need a fork lift."

"It's a mistake," I said. He shook his head and handed me the paper work that showed my husband's name and address.

"I better call him," I said. By now I was angry. Why couldn't Ted tell me he'd ordered this? A year before the smoker arrived, I'd received a call about a whiskey barrel being delivered from Tennessee. I hung up, thinking it was a crank call. It wasn't. Ted had ordered a huge whiskey barrel on wheels for cooking. The barrel was small compared to the smoker.

I called Ted. "There's a truck driver with a smoker. He says we need a fork lift."

Ted works as an effects animator. When I call him at work, he's agreeable unless he's working on a difficult scene. This wasn't a good day. "You deal with him," he said.

I wasn't feeling especially understanding. "O.K." I said, "I won't accept delivery. I'll tell him to take it back."

"Tell him to wait. I'll be home in ten minutes," Ted said. He arranged for a fork lift. The smoker was put in our driveway near our kitchen. When I looked at it, I thought it was like having a steel elephant, an 1100 pound one, outside the kitchen window.

Ted had talked to me about wanting the smoker. I had suggested getting a smaller one. No more was said. He just forgot to tell me he'd ordered it. He tends to be secretive about his purchases which is difficult for me since I'm the one dealing with the delivery people.

Returning from the store the next Saturday afternoon, I saw two fire engines in front of our house. Later I found out that when he had fired up the smoker, billowing smoke came out, filling our house and setting off the fire alarm. Thinking our house was on fire, our next door neighbor called 911.

He couldn't use it in the driveway. "Where do you think it should go?" he asked. I wanted to say, "Back to Oklahoma," but didn't. Instead I vaguely waved to a corner of our back yard. I regretted not being more specific.

Coming home Sunday, I found Ted in the back yard busily digging out plants. "My English garden," I screamed. For two years, I'd been nurturing delicate flowers in a sheltered corner of our yard. I'd made special soil mixtures and watered often. It was a spot I visited when I wanted peace. It made me feel good to see my fragile flowers growing. They were all gone.

"You told me I could put it here," he said. The smoker sat on top of freshly turned soil that had been my special garden's home. "I thought they were weeds," he said. I sputtered and cried. He apologized. But I didn't forgive him for a long time.

"I'll help you. We can put your garden somewhere else," he said. That didn't make me feel any better. The area had been carefully chosen for light and shelter. There weren't other places like that in our yard.

The smoker's been in that spot ever since. Ted bought an old Disneyland bench to sit on while the meat cooks. Sometimes he gives meat as a gift, other times he sells it at work. His love of the smoker hasn't dimmed. He enjoys the long process of choosing the finest cuts of meat, seasoning and preparing them for cooking. He buys special almond and apple wood for the fire. He enjoys the time spent in the back yard and the compliments he receives on his ribs, turkeys, and roasts.

I still need a place to grow a new garden with fragile flowers. I need to protect that place. I've waited to try again because I haven't wanted to be vulnerable.

I've learned to be more direct in communicating and to let him know specifically if something is important to me. Over time my feelings changed about the smoker. First anger, then more understanding, finally acceptance and peace came. I see how much it means to him, how much relaxation and pleasure it brings to his life.

It fits nicely in its shaded, sheltered spot. No one would know except me that once a pretty English garden grew there.

THE TRUST THING

By Hillary Krieger

Sitting in the junkie little Thai restaurant in Palm Springs, I spoon more rice onto my plate. Not much, just a teaspoon or so. I look at my husband, Stu.

"See this, it's happening. Seconds. It's the first crack in the dam."

"No, it's not. When are you going to find out about maintenance?"

The unfriendly waiters bustle around us. The air is filled with the smells of spicy beef and lemon grass. I suck down the icy cold diet coke.

"I will, I will. I promise I will."

Maintenance. I'm avoiding it the way a drug addict avoids rehab, like a drunk avoids AA. But I have to face it. I have to go to a Weight Watcher Meeting and confess that I'm terrified to eat more food. Afraid that a few more morsels will instantly put the lost weight back on. They'll understand. We speak the same insane language. That's why I go.

"I'm thinking of getting a job there." Stuart looks surprised, actually it's a miracle he didn't choke on his kung pao chicken. My uttering the word "job" in reference to myself is equivalent to saying I want to go on the next civilian shuttle launch to the moon.

"Didn't I tell you?"

"No," he sputters. "Get a job at Weight Watchers?"

"Yeah, gee, I thought I told you. I wonder why I didn't tell you."

"Why?"

"Why didn't I tell you?"

"Why do you want to work at Weight Watchers?"

"Because everybody who works there seems to keep their weight down. There's no fattys working at Weight Watchers. I think it's part of the deal, they have to stay on maintenance to keep the gig."

I diligently work to get three grains of rice between my chop sticks.

"I know why I didn't tell you."

"So?"

"If I told you, if I said it out loud, I would feel more compelled to follow through. Otherwise, I'd feel like a big loser. You know, all talk."

Why am I telling him this? I don't want him to know everything. If he knows everything, he won't love me anymore. He'll figure out that I'm nuts and split. I can't stop myself.

"If I get a job there and it works out, I'd like to become a speaker. I think I could put a new spin on the whole show. I've never heard a speaker talk about sex or alcohol in a Weight Watchers meeting. These are important issues when you're losing weight. And I think the leaders write their own agendas. It would be like having a weekly column, only I'd deliver it in person."

"Why don't they talk about alcohol? People drink."

"I know. I never want to bring it up because it makes me feel like the bad girl or something. I can't rabble rouse at Weight Watchers."

"I guess there's gotta be one place."

"I could enlighten people to a lot of tricks about drinking," I say chewing on my calorie free ice.

"There's zero points in spicy V8 and diet Coke. Bingo, a Bloody Maria and Cuba libre."

"You're just like Louis Pasteur."

"Totally. I can tell people how to scrimp on food, eat low points so they can knock a couple back on the weekend. It's bad enough watching everything you eat without giving up liquor, too."

"Amen, sister."

"It feels like some dirty little secret. Like something you just don't do."

"Is sex the other dirty little secret?"

"Yes," I say waving my chopstick. "Do you know how many people have asked me if sex is better now since I've lost weight?"

"How many?"

"I don't know. A lot. I tell them, 'How can sex be better?' What do they think, I'm a different size up my lala? I don't even know how to answer that question. I just say, 'Well, sex was always good.' Don't you think that's a weird question?"

Silence. Stu looks at me across the table.

"Stooey, what are you thinking?"

"We fit better."

"Really?"

"Yeah, like puzzle pieces that fit. It's even more right now. You know what I mean?"

I have to take a moment. Is he right? I flash my mind to when we're in bed together. By, George, he is right. There's a certain lingering now. He strokes my body more when we talk, when we have foreplay. His hands pause on the new curves and hollow places. I no longer feel ashamed of my body when we're together. I undress before I dive beneath the covers; throw my clothes off in candle light instead of making the room dark as a tomb before lovemaking. The loss of weight has been so gradual, I didn't notice that things had changed in the most intimate part of my life.

"You're right, Stooey. It is better. And thanks for not stating the obvious."

"Which obvious?"

"That sex is better now because when I get on top I don't squash you like a grape."

"I never minded turning blue."

"What a gent."

"When do you want to do this—the enlightening the world thing?"

I can tell he thinks it's a crazy scheme. Or maybe it's me who thinks it's crazy and I'm projecting it onto my poor, unsuspecting husband.

"Does it freak you out to think of my having a job?"

"I don't know if freaked out is the right word. I mean, let's face it, we've had a lot of freedom because of your being at home."

"Yeah, it's been great. Maybe I'm just thinking ahead because of the kids growing up. It won't be long until we're alone."

"It's going by too fast." He rubs his face and looks down at the table. Stooey always gets so sad when he thinks about the kids growing up and leaving.

"I'm just kicking ideas around. I don't have time for a job. On second thought, let's forget about the whole thing. I think it's safer for me to just be at home." Oh, no, what am I doing? Don't go there, don't go there.

"Why?"

"It's just a better idea for me not be around a lot of people." That really sounds crazy. I might have to confess what I really think will happen. Was there sodium pentathol in the larb? I'll try to tap dance my way out of this conversation.

"I don't want to form any new relationships. Remember what happened when I was PTA President? I'll just get into trouble."

"What kind of trouble?"

Oh, just spit it out. He already knows my whole family and hasn't left me.

"I'm afraid I'll have an affair." Well, that was good. Of all the people to tell.

"Why do you think that?" He doesn't look freaked out. His voice sounds relaxed.

"Because my ego is weak. I still want men to find me desirable. There I said it. I'm just a whore. A sickening whore. After all these years of being happily married, I'm still pathetically weak."

"You underestimate yourself. People who have affairs put out a vibe. You don't put out a vibe."

Stu never even put his chopsticks down. He's so secure. What happened to him? I stare across the table. If he just told me that he was afraid to do something out in the world because he would be tempted to have an affair, I'd probably have thrown the curried green beans in his face and run sobbing out of the restaurant.

"You're right. I don't put out a vibe. Is that why nobody flirts with me?"

"Probably. Nobody ever flirts with me, either."

"And you're cute."

"I'm adorable."

"That makes me feel better. I'm glad I confessed."

"Me, too."

What a relief. Stooey was right. I have no desire to be with other men. The thought of it is terrifying and sickening to me. What was I thinking? It's one thing not to trust other people, but to not trust yourself seems pretty ridiculous. Saying it out loud put it instantly into perspective. I lean across the table and whisper to my husband.

"It almost seems that since I'm not obsessed with my weight anymore . . ."

"But you are obsessed with your weight."

"Don't be picky. It takes less time to obsess about keeping my weight off than it does for me to just hate myself because I feel like a hog. But anyway, this lack of trust thing, these obsessions, fears. They all seem to be floating to the top. Like cream. Hmm, cream."

The cranky waiter puts the bill down without asking if we want anything else. Lucky for us we don't. We pay the bill and walk out into the cold desert night. The sky is black and clear, loaded with stars. As we stroll silently I wonder how Stuart and I could be so different. He's calm, settled. Non-judgmental and secure in the things he believes. As I fly around in a state of permanent self-doubt, he pulls me back to earth.

"Why doesn't it make you nervous when I tell you I'm afraid I'll have an affair if I walk out the front door?"

"I don't think you would."

"Why not?"

"Because I trust you."

OURS

By Janet Smith

This is a day for remembrances. The rain is streaking against the brown fence slats and the delicate green shoots of the ancient tree behind it. The tree belongs to my next door neighbor, and its age and size give the yards where it spreads shade in the hot months, scarlet bottle-brush blooms and plenty of leaves to rake up. It's trimmed every few years and still its leaf laden branches provide a wonderful backdrop of green, pierced by the knobby, brown-black, bent and scarred limbs. I see this tree in its total rugged expanse every time I come in through the front gate, and my eyes fasten on it as I walk back to the fourth door, which is ours. Yes, "ours" even though I am really the only one living in number 4. Lately, I've noticed this tree has more empty branches than leaf laden. In fact, it is looking a bit unhealthy in some areas with absent or yellow leaves at the same time the tender new buds are just visible against the gray sky.

Living and dying are the cycle of cells in the nature we know. When one you love is moving toward, or gone beyond the dying cycle, it can be a long time before this natural progression can become a living part of one's own life. It has been two and a half years since my husband died. We had reached a stage in our relationship of complete acceptance of each other with all our faults and quirks. The old arrows of jealousy he hurled at this point, I met with equal vehemence. His lack of financial success no longer mattered. The future was not part of the picture. We simply lived day to day.

Unexpected blooms of luminescent lavender, gold and vermilion orchids, plants that we had brought from Chicago gave us great pleasure. Our collection of Bach, Mozart, especially flute and guitar records expanded the time we were sharing. Cool Jazz syncopated our bodies, subtly slipping into the rhythm of our remaining life together. When I came in the lower door from the garage after work, I could count on the pungent smells of garlic, onions softened with bay leaf, thyme, rosemary, browning meat if he was feeling well enough. And he would always say, "Is that you I hear?" I always replied, "No." A drink with tinkling ice cubes awaited me. His mouth was so soft to kiss. For several years this was the high point of my work day life. As I write this that tightening feeling of being pierced by a silver shaft, an intense longing to go back, to see, to feel, hear and smell that time makes my aloneness unbearable. And then my eyes rest on the tiny buds sparkling with raindrops, the sadness is still with me but the loneliness is easier.

When our youngest son stopped overnight a few weeks ago, we were talking. I said to Dan:

"Every day I see Dick's notes—recipes in cookbooks, lists of plants bought at greenhouses, lists of prescriptions, things to save, things to pay, rubber-banded bank statements, paid bills. The desk is full of his hand written scraps of paper."

"My God! I do the same thing. I'd forgotten. I've got lists all over the place. Even though I'm right handed, we both have that small printed script. And I save all kinds of stuff, just like he did."

"It's that perfectionist idea if you have everything on paper, that's as good as doing it. You can keep it all, no choices have to be made." Dan nodded.

On Saturday night I was at our daughter Jennifer's house. We were celebrating her husband Brent's 46th birthday. There was a rap on the front door and our oldest son came in. As he took off his jacket, I noticed his gray slacks and shirt were very flattering, so I said, "Have you lost weight, Eric?" He gave me a quizzical expression, shook his head and continued on. Jen said, "Mom, he looked exactly like Dad—that expression." And she was right.

Our middle son, David, blonde as Dick was dark, looks nothing like him but he's becoming as fascinated with art and antiques as his dad was. His two year old son, Andrew, loves to throw, catch and play with all kinds of balls. Dick loved football and played on a championship high school team.

Life and death are just stages of the same journey. And death at first is a vivid loss to the living. As I am sitting here alone writing this, surrounded by everything that was part of our life, I know how happy Dick must be. Michigan won the Rose Bowl, I got our Eames chairs repaired, I fought the company where I'd worked for fifteen years that treated me unfairly and I can even put gas in the car. I miss him dearly and tears alone have such a hopeless feeling. If I could really bend time as the theorists about space propound, I would go back a ways.

For now, the rain has stopped and it's too dark to see the window, but I know there are wonderful rain-soaked plants, trees, and flowers outside that have been nourished by the dying flora that came before them. My neighbor's yard has always been a small wilderness with its big tree, wild grape vines, wandering shrubs, fuchsias, pinks, and oranges. How very beautiful each stage of the natural cycle is. It is a journey we all share.

CHAPTER SEVEN

Body

In "Stairclimb to the Top," Brooke Anderson writes about her foot race up one thousand five-hundred steps to the top of the Library Tower in Los Angeles, a piece she wrote in response to an assignment I gave one fall on "harvest." Brooke notices the other runners and queries the reader and herself about who these people are who put themselves through such physical rigors. Written in present tense, she gives the reader a very intimate view of what the runner, who has diabetes, faces each moment in terms of fluctuating sugar levels, an added challenge the non-diabetic runner would never even be aware of.

"The night before the race I am extremely careful about what I eat. More cautious than usual. I need to have energy. I awaken at 3 a.m. with my heart pounding, a sure sign of low blood sugar. I pop two glucose tablets into my mouth, put a pillow over my head and try to think of nothingness."

Brooke's style allows the reader to join her on every step of her climb. The tension of the piece builds as she runs not only because of her subject matter but because of her sentence structure and conversational style. Her sentences are short and lean.

"The fog has lifted. Without thinking I look up to the top and instantly my body fills with fear. The building appears to be extraordinarily high. I cannot do this. I must do this. I feel like I am about to be shot out of a cannon."

The reader cares whether or not Brooke will make it to the top. Whenever she reads this piece aloud, every listener in the audience responds viscerally. When she was writing the piece, she re-experienced the race. "My heart beat faster, I could feel the tension in my body, my hands began to sweat a little. I even stopped while writing to test my blood to see of the sugar levels had dropped."

The writing of this memoir helped Brooke appreciate the enormous challenge she overcame in running and completing the race and gave her a sense of pride in what she did. "It is my own Mt. Everest," she reflects, "and a personal measure that one can accomplish a goal despite adversity." This is the healing power of memoir, not only for the writer but for the reader as well. Brooke's courage gives us hope—if she can run seventy-five flights up to the top of the tallest building in Los Angeles, what can we do?

The next piece in this section is less heroic. I wrote "My Belly" with a certain tongue-in-cheek outrage and betrayal; the outrage a middle-aged woman feels when betrayed by her expanding waistline. My belly became a character in this memoir with an appetite of her own and my new alter-ego, Baubo, the ancient Greek wise woman of the "Homeric Hymn to Demeter," got into the act by basically telling me to "Get over it!" It was great fun writing this piece; humor was the only way I could approach my distress about my expanding girth.

There are few published memoirs written specifically about the body and the physical changes we all experience as we age. Mary Karr writes about her emerging sexuality as an adolescent in *Cherry*; Jean-Dominique Bauby writes about the loss of the use of his body in his forties due to "locked-in syndrome" in *The Diving Bell and the Butterfly*; and Nuala O'Faolain writes about middle-age, sexuality, and loneliness in *Are You Somebody?* But genuine appreciation for one's body is an art form that needs more attention.

In "The Obligation of Ablutions," Bairbre Dowling does just that as she remembers her mother's body while watching the care with which Korean daughters wash their mothers' backs in the Beverly Hot Springs. Bairbre reflects, "This place used to be one of those best kept secrets of Hollywood. An unemployed actor/ actress, especially with a young tireless child, could spend most of the day there for $15. It was like going on holiday."

Bairbre muses about what it would be like to soap her mother's strong swimmer's shoulders and pour water over her back while swapping gossip and telling tales about her own young daughter, named Brenda in her honor. But Bairbre will never get a chance to do that because her mother was killed in a thoughtless accident by a motorcyclist when she was Bairbre's present age.

This piece began with Bairbre's image of the bathers. "I get a visual image And then I write into the image. I hardly ever know where it is going to take me. I saw the younger women wash the strong solid bodies of older women. I longed for my mother, for her physical presence, to do something for her, something practical and pleasurable." Thoughts of her mother led her to her grandmother and then to her great-grandmother. "I wanted to make them live with me, even for a moment, by writing about them."

When we write about loved ones, we bring them alive for a moment and present our recollection of them for the reader to savor. It is an act of intimate disclosure. "The Obligation of Ablutions" is written with such vivid imagery and emotional honesty that the reader can't help but identify with Bairbre's steam-filled visions and longing to be connected to these women of her family.

STAIRCLIMB TO THE TOP

By Brooke Anderson

Harvest. A time to gather. I am gathering. I am gathering myself together. This is the time of year when one gathers strength and endurance for the winter that imposes itself on us. I am gathering. I am preparing. I am readying myself for the stair climb. Every fall. It is called "Stair Climb to the Top." A big, boastful name. I tell no one. I am stretching my capabilities beyond reason. I am gathering courage to do this foolish thing again this year.

I do not know why I am terrorizing myself again. Why am I doing something so difficult? I need this justification to fill in a hole of incompleteness. Of feeling inadequate. Of not meeting some expectation or productivity level. It is proof, my proof that I can defy my diabetes. I will outsmart it. I will challenge every blood sugar level that I come across. I need something to hold onto. I need something that can define me beyond illness. A different way to measure myself.

To get ready for the climb to the top I practice three to four times a week for several months. I find a set of weathered stairs cradled in a side of a mountain in Santa Monica. One hundred and sixty eight steps. Eight stories. I need to practice only going up but that is not possible. The stair climb is up only. Seventy-five flights. One thousand five hundred steps. The tallest building in Los Angeles. The Library Tower.

I sit in my car gathering my energy to begin a practice round. I shove the seat back in order to have enough room to change. Lifting my skirt discreetly, I squeeze into black stretch pants. I pull on my socks and running shoes and tie the laces in a tight double bow so they will not distract or cause a fall. I have a tee shirt hidden under my sweater. I strap on my running watch, test my blood, as I must always do before exercise and slowly get out of my car. I am never in a hurry to start. I carry a bottle of water, often warm from the long car ride. I stretch for a few seconds to lessen the guilt of sore muscles afterwards and I begin the descent. I must look down at each step to keep my balance. I try to pick up the pace to get the heart rate moving but know this is not necessary as going up works the heart muscle way past its ability. I am at the bottom without much effort and without stopping I start the round trip up. Stopping makes it difficult to begin again. It is slow, the climb up cannot be done fast. The first three sets are the most grueling. All I can think about is how difficult it is. I try to count and breathe. I focus on my breath. Nothing works. One step at a time. One set at a time. How many sets have I promised myself today? Can I meet the self-imposed harsh schedule?

I try to find distractions during practice on the stairs. I look at sweat drops from other climbers that appear on the wooden steps. I glance occasionally at the people. We have all sizes and ages and clothes on. I wonder what others are thinking about and why so many wear headphones. Why the constant need to hide from thought? Who is ill, suicidal or depressed? Who is having financial problems or marital strains? Who is not in turmoil? Nothing shows on the stairs. People go up and down and up and down with a variety of styles. An occasional climber carries a bicycle. Someone hops on one foot. Some take on two stairs at a time. Some run, some walk fast. Some grab the wobbly wood railing to help stall the pain of continuing. Legs are fat and skinny and in between. Stretch pants momentarily hide the flaws.

The stairs never get easier. However, with each practice round I know that I am closer to feeling a little better about myself. I do not always feel well before, during or after exercise. Exercise makes blood control even more of a challenge. The sugar range can go all over the place. If there is not enough injected insulin on board and the sugar level is high before exercising then the sugars may be even higher after a workout. High sugars slow the system. Muscles are not getting the necessary energy into their cells. The stair climb then feels like torture. The body feels depleted. It is hard to tell if the sugar is rising or falling during exercise. It is always a guess. Every day is a surprise.

I exercise fervently for weeks before the big "Stair Climb." I am possessed. I tell no one why my schedule is so busy. Only my family knows and they ignore my anxiety. I know I can climb to the top, I have done it before but can I do it this time? I ask the question a thousand times a day. The week of the event I stretch and breathe obsessively. I continue the stair practice. I time myself. I do ten round trips that equal eighty stories. I feel fat and stiff. My legs are not at all limber. They weigh me down. Nothing bends.

The night before the race I am extremely careful about what I eat. More cautious than normal. I need to have energy. I awaken at 3:00 a.m. with my heart pounding, a sure sign of low blood sugar. I pop two glucose tablets into my mouth, put a pillow over my head and try to think of nothingness. Sleep does not arrive. All I can do is rest. I get up at 6:00 a.m. and find my blood test to be 63. Incredibly low. I feel horrible, tired, jittery, nauseated. I eat, inject insulin, shower and talk myself into feeling better because no matter what, I am going to do the stair climb. I am frantically disappointed that I am not feeling well.

I drive to the race through the fog and dim light, through the colorful Korean and Hispanic sections of the city. I am ready to collapse. I am angry that my body continues to let me down.

Inside me calls an ugly little voice telling me that I am not capable, that I have no right to be doing this with my sporadic health. With great force I breakaway from these thoughts and tell myself over and over that I can do this. I repeat these words until I reach the parking structure of the downtown destination.

I park the car and walk two blocks to the start of the race. I am standing at the bottom of the building. I know from experience not to look up. My knees buckle when I do. It is cold and windy. My sweatshirt blocks some of the chill. There are not many people around except volunteers from the YMCA. I have reached the oldest age category. There are not many contestants in this bracket. We have the privilege of starting first. I check in and am relieved to know that I am on the list. I worry that my entry form has been lost in the mail. I do not want to argue. It is way too early for a confrontation.

I take another blood test. It reads 150. I am pleased. This is an ideal number for exercise. I begin to relax a little about the blood sugars. I chat with the other stairclimbers. We are an odd looking group. No one looks particularly athletic. Mostly we look tired and old. No flashy clothes. No black leather shorts. No tattoos. Just an assortment of worn gym clothes. We have our paper race numbers safety pinned on the front of our tee shirts and a yellow timer strung through our tennis shoe laces. The timer is something new. I have reservations about how I tied mine on so I do it several times to make sure it is facing downward as instructed or the time will not be accurate. No record of actually having done the climb will exist. The time disc seems to be loose and floppy and I am concerned it will be a distraction. Anxiety is gathering.

"Fifteen minutes to starting time," an announcement is made over the loud speaker. Time for one last blood test. 158, still good. My doctor suggested injecting two units of regular insulin just prior to the race because as the adrenaline kicks in, the sugar rises. I do not trust her system. I must make a quick decision since everyone is lining up. I inject a half of a unit, stuff my sweatshirt and car keys into a plastic storage bag and get in line. The fog has lifted. Without thinking I look up to the top and instantly my body fills with fear. The building appears to be extraordinarily high. I cannot do this. I must do this. I feel like I am about to be shot out of a cannon.

The music starts up, our names are announced one at a time. I run through the balloon arch to the bottom of the stairwell. I begin the ascent. The stairs look different than last year. They turn to the left and then quickly to the right. I do not remember this. Of course they have not changed. Focus and just climb. Settle down. I think I stop thinking. I begin breathing a little too strenuously. Someone in front of me is very slow but it is tricky to pass because I need to quicken my pace to get by her and that kind of exertion is difficult. I speed up and then find I am breathing too hard again. I pass three others and am feeling smug but know the feeling is temporary. I encounter a heavyset woman holding onto the railing at the eleventh floor. She is never going to make it. "You all right?" I ask. What a stupid question. What difference would it make? How could I help her?

I needed to move on to keep my pace and finish at a decent time. I tried not to look at the black numbers painted on the wall of each floor. I could not bear to see that I was only on the eighteenth floor when I was already feeling drained and doubtful. I looked anyway and often. At the twenty fifth floor I thought I was in trouble, only a third of the way through and my legs were beginning to tighten. I was grateful that I carried a water bottle. I sipped throughout the climb. As my breathing became more difficult I found the water a great comfort. I had passed five people but now others were passing me. I stepped close to the handrail as others went by. Ahead of me a hog of a man was stretched out with his arms across the entire stairwell attempting to catch his breath. I needed to get by him but it seemed not possible. Move over you selfish person I wanted to say to him but I had no extra energy at this point. He finally did move aside as I came within his view.

At last the fiftieth floor. I glanced at my stopwatch and in my nervousness I forgot to start it when I began the climb. I really needed to know my time as I was obsessed with breaking my previous record and I needed to know how to pace myself for the last third of the race. I tried not to allow this mistake to discourage me. At the fifty-fifth floor a volunteer manning her station was reading a passage from the Bible. "What does it say?" I inquired, as I kept moving. She read out loud an inspirational sentence that I could not retain or now recall but it kept me going for another few flights.

The stairwell was disorienting and dusty. My mind was filled with thoughts that would evaporate just as they were being formed. I could feel an occasional sharp pain in my lungs. A day in the coal mines. The stairwell took a turn and threw off my pace. For sixty-six flights we had been turning to the right now we had to climb to the left. A big adjustment. No choice. I tried not to think about getting close to the finish. I was determined not to look around to see how the others were doing. I concentrated on taking one step at a time. It was a large task. My mind and body were overloaded. I had planned to sprint to the top but I had nothing left in me. I continued to the 72nd floor, then the 73rd. I heard loud music and great cheering. The 74th and finally the 75th floor. Yes, I had done it. I finished. I was outside on the deck on top of the tallest building in Los Angeles. In fresh air.

I felt rotten. Something was wrong. I sat down, grabbed a towel, and reached into my fanny pack to take out my blood meter, strips and lancet. 274 was the blood test result. A normal person would test between 70 and 110. Diabetes had interfered. The disease had gotten a foothold and robbed me of feeling strong, healthy and athletic. What a huge disappointment. I do not have the ability to control glucose levels even though I sometimes pretend I can. The high sugars made me feel extremely fatigued and nauseated. No wonder I was breathing hard. My lungs felt shredded. My head ached. I drank the rest of my water and injected three units of insulin. I could not celebrate. Where was the moment of joy? Simply finishing did not seem to matter, not then anyway.

I walked down a few flights and took the elevator to the 66th floor. The victory floor. A group was gathering. We were waiting for the results to be posted. While standing in the crowd I began to calm down and let the fact that I finished to sink in. I wrapped the prize, a large loud tee shirt, around my sweaty body and paced the cement floor while viewing the enormous city below. The results were finally in. I did the climb in twenty-three minutes, not my personal best. Not at all what I had hoped for. I got into the elevator and walked to my car in a glum mood. I drove home in silence.

My daughter called. "So Mom, how did you do?"

"Not great." I replied. "I wanted to be faster. If I did not have diabetes I would have done it so much better."

To which my wise daughter replied, "If you didn't have diabetes, you probably would not have climbed the stairs at all."

She gathered me back together.

When I drive east, towards downtown on a clear day in Los Angeles, the Library Tower stands as a giant among the other buildings. Every time I see that building I feel triumphant in knowing that for a brief moment I had conquered the fear of the stairs and the craziness of diabetes. I climbed to the top. I completed the task.

MY BELLY

Maureen Murdock

I never thought I would be burdened by a belly. My flat stomach was always my badge of pride. In adolescence and young adulthood I loathed my ample thighs and full buttocks but when I put my hand on my stomach I found a firm level resting place. I didn't mind catching a side glimpse of myself in the full length hall mirror. My taut midsection profile was fine.

But then my belly began to swell. And it wasn't the mother-space that blossomed. Slowly, so I didn't notice at first, the elasticized waistbands on my pants and skirts began to leave lines. Raw, red indentations. A small mound began to grow around my navel rising like an ancient Celtic tumulus grown over with grass. It is not part of my familiar landscape; it doesn't belong. It has taken on a life of its own.

It craves bread, loves wine, yearns for chocolate. Its will bends mine. It seduces me into thinking it is invisible but my hand at rest knows otherwise.

My belly has betrayed me. She has become a harridan, demanding to be filled. She won't hold herself back another moment, not she. Her emptiness cries out to be heard. I fill her to stave off her lament of lost fertility. It is time for others to carry new life.

But then Baubo, the baudy wise woman who made Demeter laugh in her deepest grief, calls out to me. The bellywoman of the Greek daemons reminds me that a flat stomach may win Oscars but wise humor heals the heart. "Being taughtly girded is for girls," she jibes. "A bulging mid-line doesn't have to mean the end of your allure. Swing your hips, flaunt your girth, enjoy your seductiveness. Learn the art of being a wise fool."

Her words soothe me—but only to a point. Somehow I don't believe that she ever looked in the mirror. She never had to squeeze her pear shape into jeans. After all, isn't she but an archetype? And genderless at that? Baubo, I still get on the scale, look in the mirror with disdain, and hide my swelling tumulus from my lover. She laughs, "Foolish woman! Your life on this earth is too short to abide others' images!"

I'd love to be more evolved at this stage of life but I'm afraid I'm not. I find nothing redeeming about this bulging belly. It reminds me of having crossed the threshold into mid-life's netherworld. This territory is darkened by the culture's perceptions. What happened to my ripe sexuality? To the feeling of always being a girl, anticipating? If I embrace this Baubo likeness I'm afraid that I will lose the promise of some new love waiting around the corner. I'm not ready for that yet.

THE OBLIGATION

OF ABLUTIONS

By Bairbre Dowling

In the dark grotto of the Beverly Hot Springs I have watched the way people wash their bodies. Korean women washing each other. Over and over. Scrubbing, rubbing, dousing with water. Buckets and face cloths. Energetically, as if every part of their mothers—for it seemed daughters washed mothers, maybe in gratitude for the early years of washing and bathing as babies— as if every part of the skin had something in need of removal.

That scene in "Silkwood" where the woman in the shower tries to scrub off the radiation. She rubbed until it felt sore to watch even and the painful knowledge that we knew she was never going to get if off anyway.

I hope it is more than obligation that brings daughters to vigorously wash and ladle water on their mothers at Los Angeles' only naturally occurring hot springs. I wish I could wash my mother's body with its muscular vitality. Soap her broad swimmer's shoulders. Let the rinsing water flow down her narrow, muscled back over her tiny waist and saggy bum, just like mine is, her same age now. The age I still saw her naked running around the house in a hurry. Ironing her silk scarf or shirt to go out. Bathed and talced. Leaving clouds of powder as she pulled tights over her dancer's legs, beautifully defined calf muscles, a sign of intelligence she always said. I want to sit with her in the steam room, too, and talk. Watch how she loved that heat, how her always tired body relaxed in the heat. Watch her enjoying living in her body. Comfortable naked, her red hair pulled back now because of the hot steam and the tendency to fuzz up.

We could stretch out, each on our own side of the steam room and I could tell her about Brenda, her namesake. And how I'm learning Chinese, just like she took up German when I was in Senior school. I'd laughingly tell her I notice that I'm more in her position now. I need to sit up in bed at night late, like she did, and do my homework. Struggle to learn each word painstakingly, not with that disdainful ease I learned German, mocking her diligence. That osmosis learning that happens when you feel it is your due, it will come, why shouldn't it.

Then we could float together in the sulphurous pool. Plunge into the cold one. Scream. Dry each other with fluffy white towels and hug and cuddle and dry our hair and get dressed out of our lockers. Maybe we could put on make-up and powder and go hear jazz like when we heard Bill Evans together in The Vanguard when she came to see me in New York City.

I wish I could introduce her to the music of young pianist Brad Meldau and we would be in ecstasy together and maybe we'd both fall for double bass players . . . .

And we'd look at each other and say: We are both alone. At the same age. Mothers alone. With wonderful daughters.

She could never have washed her mother, she never saw her naked. It might even be true that her mother never saw herself naked.

Although she (my granny) washed and cared for her bedridden mother for years.

Yes an obligation.

CHAPTER
EIGHT

Reflections

W e end *Monday Morning Memoirs* with a section that features our wise women, our septuagenarian memoirists. Who better to reflect on their lives than those who have lived the longest and had the most life experience?

"On Pain of Death" sounds a foreboding tone but Ruth Bochner's opening sentence, "I had to wait until Jane died to get her mustard recipe" gives the reader a sly taste of what is to follow. Ruth describes the universal trait of coveting a dear friend's cherished secret; in this case, the ingredients of her hot and sweet mustard. As I have written before, no incident is too small to write about in memoir because you never know where it is going to take you. The reader discovers that the ingredients of the recipe serve as a metaphor for Jane's life; the writer discovers her own reluctance to share a recipe whose acquisition involved such a long period of patience. "This came as a mild shock to the writer," Ruth said.

When Ruth, whom we lovingly call Dr. Ruth, first read this piece to the group, she sweetened the listening by bringing each one of us a small pot of the gooey treat. Like Ruth Reichl, who included recipes in her memoir, *Tender at the Bone*, Dr. Ruth has a flair for combining the key ingredients of storytelling—character, place, and drama—into this delightful memoir. You will also see what a wily wise woman Ruth is. If this book is a great success, we'll start marketing Ruth's Mustard!

Janet Smith wrote "Dearest Richard" after we read Alice Walker's letter to her young husband in *The Way Forward is with a Broken Heart*. I had suggested to Janet that she write her memoir in letter form to her deceased husband, Richard. She enters her reminiscence about their romance of fifty-two years ago through the wet atmosphere of the day. "Whenever the day is gray, rainy, and deeply dreamy, why do I dwell on our life so?"

We all envy Janet's clear memory for details and nuance of feelings as she describes the aching yearning young lovers have when they are separated by time and distance. To the young lover who becomes her husband she writes: "We'd just get to the comfort of being together and you'd have to leave." Rather than being maudlin, Janet's intimate style allows the reader to reminisce about his or her own first love and the excitement of starting a life together at twenty-two.

Dorothy Huebel's "Memories of Romance" also addresses romantic love but her memoir is a fairy tale with a different perspective—what happens after "happily ever after." Dorothy writes to the reader: "Once upon a time, long long before Viagra, when you used to dress for bed, you quivered at the thought of being undressed, of running your fingers through his full head of hair, and you tingled in anticipation of the magic touch of his musculature." No, this is not X-rated; quite the contrary. Dorothy carefully gives the reader a lesson in time travel, a very important tip for a memoir writer. How you establish both past time (then) and present time (now) in the same piece is where the craft of memoir writing gets honed.

Dorothy sets the past in a time "long long before Viagra" and the present in a description of a ritual of present-day love. "Now, though you still dress for bed, you have in all probability replaced the peek-a-boo gowns that clung to those perky, pink, little button-tipped mounds with pajamas that mask the deflated balloons clinging to your rib cage . . . ." She ends the piece with a self-reflection, another key element of memoir writing, which extols the comforts of a long-lived love. "Do not look back. And, for heaven sakes, do not look too far forward, just concentrate on the positives of here and now. You have a man, you have a bed, you have pajamas, and you have a secret you can cherish for the rest of your life." You'll have to read her piece to discover what that secret is.

In "Two Weeks in Madrid, 1984" Ruth Bochner, now in her seventies, reflects on her feelings at midlife. She had the opportunity to accompany her husband to Madrid while he was working on a film and to witness first-hand the changes that were occurring in post-Franco Spain. As she observes life changing for the Spanish woman of the eighties, she reflects on her own life as the spouse of an actor resuming the rigors of his work life after heart surgery. As she walks down the dark alleys of medieval Spain, she faces her own dark anxieties about her future now that her role of caregiver is no longer essential.

"As I watch the new post-dictatorship Spanish woman striding her long confident strides, tight-fitted jeans and spike-heeled boots, this new woman may kiss, may smoke on the street, may divorce now, live with a lover, become a lawyer, a policewoman, and use birth control. I also see out of the corner of my eye the 'dictator woman' in dowdy black with squat, square body, a heavy, even step and wonder if 'woman' anywhere escapes the fascist hold." Ruth's attention to detail allows the reader to absorb not only the rich sensual environment around her but also the emotional truth that lingers there. Her writing always provokes the reader to see beyond the personal to the universal experience of us all.

We end the book, as we began, with Jackie Connolly. "Wellspring" is a memoir about the place in nature Jackie has returned to for many years for renewal. As we slowly climb the rocks along the shoreline with her and listen to the ocean roar, we are gently transported by her word images to our own place of rest and renewal. With her, we watch the seemingly stationary life of the sea anemones and barnacles contrast with the gulls that soar.

"On the beach, a scattering of small pebbles lie stranded and as the tide recedes, they leave paths of their journey, etched in sand like gleaming polliwog tails . . . . This—the sand, the sky, the sea—this is my hallowed ground." Jackie writes in the tradition of Thomas Merton in *The Seven Story Mountain* and Kathleen Norris in *Dakota: A Spiritual Geography*; two memoirs that address the sacred in nature.

As she later reflected on this piece, Jackie saw it as a metaphor for her own aging process. "I guess the changes in me are subconsciously highlighted in contemplating the agelessness of the sea. I can always *depend* upon it, which I now realize is what I find so comforting and reassuring. No matter what else is happening, changing, or falling apart in my life, the security of knowing that I can anchor myself to that solid rock, look out and know the tide will come in and go out is comforting. But it is never so calm that it is tedious and predictable." Jackie gives us a sense of the universality of life as a journey.

Memoir takes the reader along the writer's journey telling him the details of her life and what she has learned along the way. The memoirist asks the reader to take the same journey of reflection about his or her life to find the treasures that may be buried below the surface of recollection. It doesn't matter how young or old you are when you begin to write about the hills and vales of your life. Just focus on an event that you want to discover more about and write with as much emotional honesty as you can muster. You will find that your life has meaning for others because we are indeed all part of the same continuum. As Jackie writes:

"Hundreds of years ago, probably thousands, some Indian woman sat on this same spot, keeping watch, absorbing strength from the sea's enduring godforce before returning to her tribe. I know that I am an integral part of that continuum, like all who came before me and all who follow. That is enough; that is all."

ON PAIN OF DEATH

By Ruth Bochner

I had to wait until Jane died to get her mustard recipe. Jane was a comedienne, a sophisticated whisky-voiced actress from New England with a flare for character. She was delightful, one generation older, a woman to be emulated who made a perfect Caesar salad with a coddled egg, who served fruit swimming in brandy in the wee hours. Her husband, Freddie, assistant headmaster of Upper Canada College for Boys, suffered the performers and then went to bed in disgust at his disturbed routine.

Jane gave her mustard recipe to Corinne, also an actress, exacting a promise from Corinne never to pass it on to anyone. In fact, one year I asked Corinne for it and the answer was a flat "NO!"

I remember the night that Corinne was rehearsing a TV show with my husband, Lloyd, and I called the studio to announce that I was en route to the hospital to deliver our third child. And now here we are four years later, Corinne with her husband, and Lloyd and I not far away, all living in Los Angeles, and I still want that recipe for Jane's mustard.

When you were ill or had a party, Corinne would bring a

small pot of it to be cherished and used sparingly until you were lucky enough to deserve another. The pots were china, or pottery, or often a tiny jar that had contained capers, now with the label "Corinne's Mustard." The mustard is hot and sweet, the ingredients so mysterious. Is it sugar or honey; is it mustard seed or dried English?

When Jane died a theater was named after her, and Corinne was one of the prime movers in raising funds to refurbish it.

"Corinne," I spoke, "Jane held me in high regard. We were friends. I loved her. She would want me to have her mustard recipe now."

"Well," Corinne said after a long pause, "maybe if Lloyd buys a seat in the theater (we'll put his name on it), I'll give you the recipe." She was pleased by the idea.

"Anyone buying a seat can have it."

"Lloyd," I said, "We need to buy a seat in Jane's theater, in memoriam. Will we?"

"Of course," he replied. "I'm sending a check. Why are you so intense about it? Why the rush?"

"Well, then I can have Jane's mustard recipe."

Now, when people ask "May I have the recipe?" after describing how it tastes on salmon, perfect on baked chicken, on roast beef sandwiches, in keeping Jane's tradition, I look with innocent horror and quietly remark, "Not even on pain of death am I allowed to share the recipe." Finally I have Jane's recipe and I make it and I give it and am always looking for perfect little pots and small jars . . . . but not from capers.

And the label reads "Ruth's Mustard."

DEAREST RICHARD

By Janet Smith

Whenever the day is gray, rainy, deeply dreamy, why do I
dwell on our life? I'm going back to your first real car, that brown
and cream Chevrolet and the time we spent in it on the week-
ends you drove from Michigan to Massachusetts.

You'd get there Saturday morning after driving all night
through Canada to Buffalo and on to Pittsfield and South Hadley.
There were no thruways then, just highways, little towns,
mountains, woods. The only room available near the college was
in a boarding house on the road not far from Abbey, my dorm
senior year. I never saw the inside of your room but it sounded
pretty dismal.

We'd have breakfast at the College Inn and if it was rainy
like today, go back to the car, drive up to the mountains and
park. It always took a while before the distance between us
disappeared. Maybe half the day. I couldn't feel close until I got
used to the real you wearing rumpled old clothes, growing a slight
beard, looking tired and anxious. It was like meeting you all over
again. Making small talk on the surface, just waiting for the
moment when your arms would naturally draw me close to you
and we could say what really mattered. How much I'd missed

you, yet I was never able to convince you that you were the only one in my life. Maybe I hadn't really convinced myself. Slowly the old mutual easiness would return.

When we drove around the Connecticut river valley, we stopped to look at the old graveyards that were next to the white-steepled churches in every little town. Many went back to Revolutionary days. The stones were dark, mossy, broken, some even lying in the overgrown grassy weeds. There were so many children who had died young. Is it the dreary day today that leads me to think of those old markers? Or that my own life is closer to its end? More likely, it is that you are no longer here to share it with me.

Remember the vivid oranges, crimsons, golds of the trees reflecting in Upper Lake when you visited in October? I'm looking at my favorite faded, cracked snapshot of you whittling a stick in those ancient, yellow corduroys and blue shirt. We were sitting on the ground by the lake. Always so serious. No one else I had ever gone out with admitted how much he liked art and classical music. When you told me you played the flute because of its pure sound, I was amazed. I'd only seen the football player, the shy guy with plenty of friends from Oak School.

I don't know which New Year's Eve it was, but you had a party in the recreation room at your house on Edgewood, the designer house built for a Life magazine project. I laid on the couch with you. You were wearing a red and black checked wool shirt. I know because you got so hot that the shirt began to smell like a wet dog. I had on a cinnamon colored sweater and a yellow wool skirt that I had traded my friend Rosemary for my blue pleated one. It was the first time you touched my breasts, on the outside of that sweater. Couples were scattered all over the house. Your parents were at a party. How shocked but impassioned I was by your groping.

But back to those college days. You bought me a record player, RCA Victor with needles that had to be changed. Remember those first records, "Sacred and Profane Dances" by

Debussy, on the back something by Ravel, the "Romanian Dances," the "Emperor Concerto" on clear red plastic? Stravinsky and Shostakovich? You couldn't come to my room but we could play records in the so-called "date room." I could have you for dinner as a guest. I don't remember a single memorable meal, but we didn't have any money. In fact, it was rare to see a movie.

I know we spent a lot of time in your car, which was pretty small. Once in a while you came up with a short bottle of bourbon and one of ginger ale. I smuggled glasses from the dining room. We both smoked by then. I've never understood how sex in the car was anything but worrisome. It never seemed to bother you. Like always, it was afterwards, with my head on your chest, my mouth pressed to the pulse in the hollow of your neck. How much in love we were.

We'd just get to the comfort of being together and you'd have to leave. I couldn't wait for graduation and our wedding in September. I often wonder if we could have just lived together in New York. Lived life as our five kids have. We could have gotten jobs, couldn't we? I would have tried to join a dance company. But your dad was literally screaming for help at his company, Brewer Sewing Supplies, so we never considered another course of action. In just over a year we had Eric. The rest you know.

We drove that same car to Colorado on our honeymoon in September 1948. Remember that first night at the Baker Hotel in St. Charles? I don't know what I expected, but the room was huge. Nothing grand, just a plain old double bed with a chenille bedspread. When I think of it now, the peach silk nightgown and negligee my mother had made for me seems touching and beautiful. The only memory I have of that night was how hot the room was. After we opened the window, the cars crossing the bridge over the Fox River seemed very loud.

Staying in hotels, as commercial as they were, seemed an exotic experience on our trip though the flat farmlands of the mid-west. The strangeness of sleeping all night in the same bed with you gradually lost its awkwardness. I pretended sleep more than I actually slept. When we finally got to the Rocky Mountains, I was overwhelmed. I'd never seen anything like those soaring peaks and plunging falls.

Remember that week in Estes Park? Why was it so important that no one suspect we were on our honeymoon? That was the first time I'd ever felt flannel sheets, but it was cold at that altitude. We rode horses on trails along the ridges and scared as I was, the magnificent mountain scenery caught me by surprise. You couldn't get enough, remembering your days at Yellowstone being a ranger during summer vacations when World War II took all the older men. You loved our stay at Estes Park. The wilder, the better. We had to leave because of the weather although we knew it before we planned our trip.

The good old Chevy took us to Colorado Springs to The Broadmoor Hotel. More my idea of a honeymoon. Here, in our separate cottage, my silky nightgown rarely came off the hook. The soft white sheets and lush towels made me relax. I wore a long dark green dress with tiny pleats to dinner where we tried our first martini—that cool smoothness warming my mouth at first sip—twirling the olive with the toothpick. You wore your beige gabardine suit and we danced to the live orchestra. I know you remember the Indian silver necklace and bracelet you bought me at The Broadmoor. I still wear them.

We were twenty-two. It's been over fifty years, but I can still see us dancing, better I can feel us dancing, your hot hand on my neck, my temple pressed against yours, our clasped hands pulled down so our bodies touched.

> "When the deep purple falls over sleepy garden walls
> and the stars begin to shimmer in the sky
> In the mist of a memory you wander back to me,
> Breathing my name with a sigh."

Remember that old popular song? When we returned, we traded that small brown and cream car for our jointly-owned Ford station wagon with the wood paneled sides and the gray Pontiac convertible. It was no longer you and me. And now after all those years it's just me.

MEMORIES OF ROMANCE

By Dorothy S. Huebel

Once upon a time, long, long before Viagra, when you used to dress for bed, you quivered at the thought of being undressed, of running your fingers through his full head of hair, and you tingled in anticipation of the magic touch of his musculature. Afterwards, when you were finally ready for sleep, you thrilled at the sound of those little purrs of love satisfied, and you fell asleep with a smile on your face, and love in your heart.

Now, though you still dress for bed, you have in all probability, replaced the peek-a-boo gowns that clung to those perky, pink, little button-tipped mounds with pajamas that mask the deflated balloons clinging to your rib cage, and the image of being undressed is hysterical. The very thought of running your fingers over his smooth, glistening pate is about as thrilling as massaging a billiard ball—and, it is far better not to even think about what happened to his musculature. It's that time of life when those endearing little purrs have turned into puffs and snorts.

So, you make one last trip to the bathroom, climb into bed and turn on your side with your back to the back of a retired magician. You put your good ear on the pillow and like nested spoons you go to sleep wrapped in the heart-warming comfort of familiarity.

Do not look back. And, for heaven sakes, do not look too far forward, just concentrate on the positives of here and now. You have a man, you have a bed, you have pajamas, and you have a secret you can cherish for the rest of your life. Who, certainly not your children, would ever believe that you used to share a bed with a master magician—a Houdini, as it were.

Best of all, however, and what really matters, is that you still have a loving companion with whom you once shared magic moments—a man who during all of your years together never once complained about keeping your cold feet warm.

TWO WEEKS IN MADRID—

1984

By Ruth Bochner

Spain is a dark country pervaded by death and suffering; a country proud in history and conquest. I had to allow that darkness to wash over me. What came from a potential joyous holiday was very different from expectations. I became the dark country but without pride in conquest or history.

Today, it is dark and raining, but our days have been warm and the evenings, mild. This trip is a gift although it all starts off badly. We are assembled at the airport where Carlos, the Spanish film producer, waits to take charge of passports, luggage and boarding passes. "Go, I take care everything," he says. "Buy duty-free, have drink." But we are missing the young leading actor. "Twenty-eight film I make and is first time I lose actor." The plane leaves forty-five minutes late with no leading man.

Carlos roams the aisles of the plane explaining his company, his basis of operation, and of the missing one he says, "Alla time the marijuan he smoke, smoke too much the marijuan this boy." After dinner he remarks, "Is no good the dinner? Is no everything can be good." Then back to his original complaint: "Twenty-eight film I make and is first time I lose actor."

Carlos is a big man and wears terrible clothes: a handmade sleeveless tunic sweater stretching to his knees in a two-toned diagonal print of dirty gray and faded black; jogging pants and a cotton jersey also in faded black and the worst decrepit sneakers. His gray-black hair is wildly bushy and melts into his gray-black beard. Only his cheeks and neck show white. His eyes, though, are warm, brown. He is altogether very loveable.

"What will you do, Carlos?" I say.

"Is big problem, no?" he answers.

His arms rise and fall slapping his sides. Well, this is not my barrel of woe. I stretch out and proceed to practice the "don'ts" of flying: I drink excellent Spanish coffee, sip cognac after wine, and begin to luxuriate in this unexpected wondrous contrast to our lives.

On arrival, out in the parking lot, Carlos looks up at the sky and says, "Is big, is beautiful, no? Is good for the pulmons. Pipils come from all places to Madrid for the pulmons." He pounds his broad chest and breathes deeply. The man loves his city.

In our apartment hotel, Lloyd and I enjoy modern comforts and a helpful staff although I always hope that when overseas we will have old cornices (even peeling ones), flowered wallpaper, quilts, a balcony, and a courtyard. Below our window is a sandy-floored park, a variety of dogs roaming free, and youngsters playing soccer. To the left is the Palace of Justice with stately columns, Roman sculpture, and a slated dome. We look out on ancient red-tiled roofs, exquisite grille-work, wooden shutters and bursting crimson sunsets, buildings of dusty yellow and burnt orange—goodness for the eye. And I begin to forgive the garbage compactor, but I refuse to push the button.

I'm easy when we travel. I'm so pleased to be here with new sounds and feelings. But at the end of the day, Lloyd comes in gray and exhausted and I think he shouldn't be working yet. It's too soon, barely seven weeks since his open-heart surgery, and a promised eight-hour day stretches to ten, then twelve. We sit sunning in the Plaza Major and try to imagine the bullfights and auto-de fe during the Inquisition, wondering what it was like to watch the burnings at the stake—bloody and cruel days.

Now a people concerned with inflation, entry into the Common Market, and their separateness from the rest of Western Europe fill the plaza. A proud heritage, a flaming empire, now eight years after Franco a government almost Communistic. A reaction to benign dictatorship. In Latin countries women do not sit alone in restaurants; it isn't seemly. Therefore I go to coffee bars and cafeterias but am aware the choice is not mine.

The time, however, is mine. I walk six or seven hours a day down new boulevards, lanes, and alleys. On one occasion I visit the tapestry factory where I watch men and women of various ages weaving rugs, appliquéing, repairing old tapestries, embroidering in gold and red the fringed banners for the House of Bourbon; intricate petit-point work for palaces and museums. And I watch the feet of the workers standing all day in carpet slippers and running shoes.

A heavy sadness comes and goes. Nothing that I conjure up. At the park, watching the children in rowboats, splashing one another with oars, and sipping espresso, it comes; sadness from the months gone by. Here, in this beautiful city filled with the new and exotic I try not to let myself be dragged down. Exploring, looking for details in old haunts, soaking in the richness as I look at paintings I have seen before at the Prado and never expected to see again.

Is this trip a watershed? No, I think we have carried the same baggage and old routines to this new place. I feel old echoes in the swirling leaves that skirt about the air this time of year, the beginning of a new season of change. But from the cracked record of the winding-down machine the music sounds hollow and there are echoes of old dreads.

Do we have to wait until spring after a long-chilled sleeping winter for the sunshine, the running sap and sweet blossoms? I want a promise that if we wait out the cold months there will be warmth from hidden shadows of all the dread. Perhaps we will find only old melodies badly orchestrated. Where once we walked with strength, compressing previous hours, jamming those hours full, distilling tastes and sounds to be tucked away and brought out later, stretched and uncreased are the memories, the pleasures now only measured steps.

The days are flying. I try to count the time here and not the time left before leaving. There is so much I want to see and do; the Sunday flea market, the tapas bars in the twisty lanes. I want to buy another pair of shoes, just the perfect pair. I want to stay in this small apartment with the marble floors, the large glazed clay pots filled with dried sunflowers, pods and wheat stalks in the hall just outside our door. I want to eat another Spanish croissant with its thin coating of honey.

Why now and here, to have the darkness consume me with leaden depression when lightness should be penetrating life? See this, see that, mark it. It's marvelous. The keeper waits the dawn and grabs her pail of cleaning materials as does the maid down the hall. The cherished child becomes the giving slave, the gifts of yore, gone. The drone stands on the mound of sand midstream wanting to stay forever the isolate, the observer of other shores. The barge left and will not return. You did not make up your mind speedily enough and so stand betwixt and between life and nothing.

I hear the milkman below the window, the clink of his bottles; but it is too dark and I am too far up to see him. If I were closer to earth, I too might have a purpose, perhaps to help him sort the bottles and feel a part of the doing world.

As I watch the new post-dictatorship Spanish woman striding her long confident strides, tight-fitted jeans and spike-heeled boots, this new woman may kiss, may smoke on the street, may divorce now, live with a lover, become a lawyer, a policewoman and use birth control. I also see out of the corner of my eye the "dictator woman" in dowdy black with squat, square body, with heavy, even step and wonder if "woman" anywhere escapes the fascist hold. It waits, I think, with offers of place and serenity in exchange for freedom and isolation that comes from veering from the common mold. Every age has those few who manage to skirt the norm. And what is gained, I do not know.

It is late for choices one never felt one had. I chose the old plodding "dictatorship" one. She knows where the lane goes, where the twists are and where it leads. She feels faceless, safe, accepted.

The last time I saw Carlos he was dressed in gray flannel, yellow cashmere, a tartan scarf hung loose about his neck. His hair was tamed, his beard trimmed. He was working, not traveling. As we kissed goodbye on both cheeks I thanked him for the two weeks in his majestic city. "Don worry, I bring you again here," he says. And looking beyond at Lloyd he nods, "Him too."

I believe him. And next time, I'll find the perfect pair of shoes.

WELLSPRING

By Jacqueline Connolly

I have loved many places in my life and they have all shared one thing in common: water. My favorite spot is up the coast where a cluster of small, sandy coves lie separated by a large outcropping of rocks that stretch from adjacent cliffs into the ocean. It is called Leo Carrillo State Park. I have romped there with my children, gathering shells and searching through tide pools; I have sought seclusion there when life's stresses threaten to overwhelm, and I have escaped there in moods of self-indulgent whimsy. Always I return to the city stronger.

This sense of renewal begins as soon as I reach the highway. I tell myself that I can just keep driving North on this road forever: to Santa Barbara, San Francisco, perhaps even Alaska! What would happen if I did? This sense of freedom is intoxicating. Once past Malibu, the commercial distractions thin out, the hillside houses are fewer, and I savor the increasing vistas of clean, blue surf.

The best time for going there is in the cool months when fewer people are around. I thrive on the solitude, the fresh, foggy smell of the salt air, fish, kelp and—I like to imagine—faraway islands. The empty life-guard towers stand like sentinels and in the sheltered coves my footprints are sometimes the only marks of intrusion as I wend my way through the sand to a section of boulders below the cliff, sheltered from the grate of cars, the tremors of civilization.

I search for a smooth spot upon which to settle, someplace where I can enjoy the teeming tide-pool life trapped between the rocks without getting soaked by spray from the breaking surf. Always the old reliables are there: barnacles in their relentless spread along with their mussel cohorts and I wonder why I can never remember which months the mussels are edible and which months they aren't, and why. Usually I find anemones and they trigger memories of the time I felt adventurous enough to eat some in Sicily. How could people consider them a treat? The bright green sea lettuce intermingled with the red algae add a delectable contrast to the otherwise muted color scheme. I wonder, does anyone eat sea lettuce?

Looking out toward the ocean, I become mesmerized by the rhythm of its sounds: a bass crescendo as waves bellow into shore, the momentary hush as they recede, slapping the rocks as they let go. And always the dissonant screech of the gulls as they graze the water's surface, rise, circle high, dive and rise again. Oh, how I envy them! The rowdy flocks fighting over dinner, the solitary ones floating apart or those who, like me, stand on rocks keeping watch. I long for their freedom to fly and swoop and scream, their ingress into hidden fissures, the ease with which they drift wherever the mood or current takes them.

By afternoon, the cold wind blows against me, forcing my hair back from my face, its purity refreshing. I linger for hours, strolling along the water's edge, moving from rock to rock. Down the shoreline I watch the slick black figures maneuver their boards around dark beds of kelp, waiting for that perfect breaker, one whose power will eclipse all others before it. Beyond them a few adventurous wind surfers skim across the surface and occasionally soar as they catch a hearty gust, while back on shore a small Asian boy discovers a gleaming strand of sea weed and, running back and forth across the sand, laughingly drags it behind him, followed by a grandfather trudging wearily behind.

On the beach, a scattering of small pebbles lie stranded and, as the tide recedes, they leave paths of their journey etched in sand like gleaming polliwog tails. Further back, larger, smooth-honed rocks are cast at random with fragments of broken shells and shreds of seaweed—all marked with the white splattering of birds. Playing tag with the surf, curlews with their narrow, down-curved beaks dig for crabs. This—the sand, the sky, the sea—*this* is my hallowed ground.

And as the sea breaks closer and its fine mist turns icy, I move further back on the rocks; they're cold and scraggy and I think a *sensible* person would bring a pillow to soften the pressure but then I remember how vital it is for me not to be "always sensible," and as I snuggle down into their crevices, I am forced to confront the changes time has wrought. I have become clumsy, no longer able to scamper down the cliffs, over the rugged outcroppings. Now I scoot awkwardly around on my seat or, like a baby learning to crawl, use my hands and knees for balance. I, the one who bragged about taking risks, who when called fool-hardy considered it a compliment, am now not only afraid of falling but convinced that if I do, something vital will break and nothing—*nothing*—will ever heal.

Never mind. Hundreds of years ago, probably thousands, some Indian woman sat on this same spot, keeping watch, absorbing strength from the sea's enduring godforce before returning to her tribe. I know that I am an integral part of that continuum, like all who have come before me and all who will follow. That is enough; that is all.

BIBLIOGRAPHY

SELECTED MEMOIR

BIBLIOGRAPHY

Abbott, Shirley. *The Bookmaker's Daughter*. New York: Ticknor & Fields, 1991.

Albom, Mitch. *Tuesdays with Morrie*. New York: Doubleday, 1997.

Alexander, Meena. *Fault Lines*. New York: The Feminist Press, 1993.

Allende, Isabel. *Paula*. New York: Harper Collins Publishers, 1994.

Barrington, Judith. *Writing the Memoir*. Portland, Or: The Eighth Mountain Press, 1997.

Barrios, Flor Fernandez. *Blessed by Thunder: Memoir of a Cuban Girlhood*. Seattle: Seal Press, 1999.

Bayley, John. *Elegy for Iris*. New York: St. Martin's Press, 1999.

Bragg. Rick. *All Over but the Shoutin'*. New York: Pantheon Books, 1997.

Chernin, Kim. *In My Mother's House*. New York: Harper & Row, 1983.

Covington, Vicki and Dennis. *Cleaving: The Story of a Marriage*, North Point Press, 1999.

Delattre, Pierre. *Episodes*. St. Paul, Minn.: Graywolf Press, 1993.

DeSalvo, Louise. *Writing as a Way of Healing*. Boston: Beacon Press, 1999.

Diski, Jenny. *Skating to Antarctica*. Hopewell, NJ: The Ecco Press, 1997.

Eggers, Dave. *A Heartbreaking Work of Staggering Genius*. New York: Vintage, 2000.

Frazier, Ian. *Family*. New York: Harper, 1994.

Gates, Henry Louis, Jr. *Colored People*. New York: Vintage, 1995.

Gordon, Emily Fox. *Mockingbird Years*. New York: Basic Books, 2000.

Gornick, Vivian. *The Situation and the Story*. New York: Farrar, Straus and Giroux, 2001.

Gornick, Vivian. *Fierce Attachments*. New York: Simon & Schuster, 1987.

Griffin, Susan. *A Chorus of Stones*. New York: Anchor Books, 1992.

Hahn, Hannelore. *On the Way to Feed the Swans*. New York: Tenth House, 1982.

Hampl, Patricia. *I Could Tell You Stories*. New York: W. W. Norton & Co., 1999.

Harrison, Catherine. *The Kiss*. New York: Avon, 1997.

Heilbrun, Carolyn G. *Writing a Woman's Life*. New York: Ballantine Books, 1988. 24 hooks, bell. *Remembered Rapture: The Writer at Work*. New York: Henry Holt & Co., 1999.

Jacobs, Harriet A. *Incidents in the Life of a Slave Girl*. Cambridge: Harvard University Press, 2000.

Jamison, Kay Redfield. *An Unquiet Mind*. New York: Alfred A. Knopf, 1995.

Kamenetz, Rodger. *Terra Infirma: A Memoir of My Mother's Life in Mine*. New York: Schocken Books, 1985.

Karr, Mary. *The Liars' Club*. New York: Penguin Books, 1995.

Ker Conway, Jill. *When Memory Speaks*. New York: Alfred A. Knopf, 1998.

_____. Ed. *Written by Herself: Women's Memoirs from Britain, Africa, Asia and the United States*. New York: Vintage, 1996.

_____. *True North*. New York: Vintage, 1994.

_____. *The Road from Coorain*. New York: Vintage, 1990.

King, Stephen. *On Writing: A Memoir of the Craft*. New York: Scribner, 2000.

Lamott, Anne. *Traveling Mercies*. New York: Random House, 1999.

_____. *Bird by Bird*. New York: Pantheon Books, 1994.

Lopate, Phillip. *The Art of the Personal Essay*. New York: Anchor Books, 1994.

Lyden, Jacki. *Daughter of the Queen of Sheba*. New York: Penguin Books, 1998.

MacDonald, Michael Patrick. *All Souls: A Family Story from Southie*. Boston: Beacon Press, 1999.

Boston: Beacon Press, 1999.

Mayer, Musa. *Night Studio*. New York: Dimensions, 1987.

_____ *Examining Myself*. New York: Faber and Faber, 1994.

McBride, James. *The Color of Water: A Black Man's Tribute to His White Mother*. New York: Riverhead Books, 1996.

Mc Carthy, Mary. *Memories of a Catholic Girlhood*. New York: Harcourt Brace Jovanovich, 1957.

McConkey. James., ed. *The Anatomy of Memory*. New York: Oxford University Press, 1996.

McCourt, Frank. *Angela's Ashes*. New York: Scribner, 1996.

_____ *Tis*. 1999.

Menchu, Ribogerta. *I, Rigoberta Menchu: An Indian Woman in Guatemala*. London: Verso, 1984.

Merriman, Andy. *A Minor Adjustment: The Story of Sarah, a Remarkable Child*. London: Pan Books, 1999.

Murdock, Maureen. *Fathers' Daughters*. New York: Fawcett, 1996.

_____ *The Heroine's Journey*. Boston: Shambhala, 1990.

Norris, Kathleen. *Dakota: A Spiritual Geography*. Boston: Houghton Mifflin, 1993.

O'Faolain, Nuala. *Are You Somebody: The Accidental Memoir of a Dubliner Woman*. New York: Henry Holt, 1996.

O'Reilly, Mary Rose. *Barn at the End of the World*. Milkweed, 2000.

Peterson, Brenda. *Sister Stories*. New York: Viking, 1996.

Rainer, Tristine. *Your Life as Story*. New York: Tarcher/Putnam, 1997.

Reichl, Ruth. *Tender at the Bone*. New York: Broadway Books, 1999.

Roberts, Cokie. *We Are Our Mothers' Daughters*. New York: William Morrow, 1998.

Andy Rooney. *My War*. New York: Public Affairs, 2000

Sarton, May. *Journal of a Solitude*. New York: W.W. Norton & Co., 1973.

See, Carolyn. *Dreaming*. New York: Random House, 1995.

Slater, Lauren. *Lying*. New York: Random House, 2000.

_____ *Welcome to My Country*. New York: Bantam Doubleday, 1994.

Tiberghien, Susan. *Circling to the Center*. Mahwah, NJ: Paulist Press, 2000.

_____. *Looking for Gold*. Einsiedeln, Switzerland: Daimon, 1997.

Walker, Alice. *The Way Forward Is with a Broken Heart*. New York: Random House, 2000.

Welch, John. *Spiritual Pilgrims: Carl Jung and Teresa of Avila*. Mahwah, NJ: Paulist Press, 1982.

Wilde-Menozzi, Wallis. *Mother Tongue*. New York: North Point Press, 1997.

Williams, Terry Tempest. *Leap*. New York: Pantheon, 2000.

_____. *Refuge: An Unnatural History of Family and Place*. New York: Vintage Books, 1991.

Wolff, Geoffrey. *The Duke of Deception: Memories of My Father*. New York: Vintage Books, 1990.

Wolff, Tobias. *This Boy's Life*. Grove Press, 2000.

Zinsser, William K., ed. *Inventing the Truth: The Art and Craft of Memoir*. New York: Houghton Mifflin Co., 1998.

TOPICAL MEMOIRS

Alcoholism

Cheever, Susan. *Note Found in a Bottle*. New York: Simon and Schuster, 1999.
Karr, Mary. *The Liars' Club*. New York: Penguin Books, 1995.
See, Carolyn. *Dreaming*. New York: Random House, 1995.

Alzheimers

Bayley, John. *Elegy for Iris*. New York: St. Martin's Press, 1999.
————. *Iris and Her Friends*. New York: W.W. Norton, 2000.

Bi-polar Disorder, Depression

Diski, Jenny. *Skating to Antarctica*. Hopewell, NJ: The Ecco Press, 1997.
F. Scott Fitzgerald, "The Crack-Up," in Lopate, Phillip. *The Art of the Personal Essay*. New York: Anchor Books, 1994.
Jamison, Kay Redfield. *An Unquiet Mind*. New York: Alfred A. Knopf, 1995.
Lyden, Jacki. *Daughter of the Queen of Sheba*. NY: Penguin Books, 1998.

Styron, William. *Darkness Visible: A Memoir of Madness*. New York: Vintage, 1992.

Cross-Dressing

Middlebrook, Diane Wood. *Suits Me: The Double Life of Billy Tipton*. New York: Houghton Mifflin, 1998.

Cultural Memoir

Allende, Isabel. *Paula*. New York: Harper Collins Publishers, 1994.

Anzaldua, Gloria. *Borderlands, La Frontera: The New Mestiza*. San Francisco: Aunt Lute Books, 1999.

Barrios, Flor Fernandez. *Blessed by Thunder: Memoir of a Cuban Girlhood*. Seattle: Seal Press, 1999.

Ker Conway, Jill, Ed. *Written by Herself: Women's Memoirs from Britain, Africa, Asia and the United States*. New York: Vintage, 1996.

_____. *True North*. New York: Vintage, 1994.

_____. *The Road from Coorain*. New York: Vintage, 1990.

MacDonald, Michael Patrick. *All Souls: A Family Story from Southie*. Boston: Beacon Press, 1999.

Boston: Beacon Press, 1999.

Menchu, Rigoberta. *I, Rigoberta Menchu*: An Indian Woman in Guatemala. London: Verso, 1994.

Down's Syndrome

Merriman, Andy. *A Minor Adjustment: The Story of Sarah, a Remarkable Child*. London: Pan Books, 1999.

Incest

Harrison, Catherine. The Kiss. New York: Avon, 1997.

In Search of the Mother

Chernin, Kim. *In My Mother's House.* New York: Harper & Row, 1983.

Kamenetz, Rodger. *Terra Infirma: A Memoir of My Mother's Life in Mine.* New York: Schocken Books, 1985.

McBride, James. *The Color of Water: A Black Man's Tribute to His White Mother.* New York: Riverhead Books, 1996.

Reichl, Ruth. *Tender at the Bone.* New York: Broadway Books, 1999.

Roberts, Cokie. *We Are Our Mothers' Daughters.* New York: William Morrow, 1998.

Williams, Terry Tempest. *Refuge: An Unnatural History of Family and Place.* New York: Vintage Books, 1991.

In Search of the Father

Abbott, Shirley. *The Bookmaker's Daughter.* NY: Ticknor & Fields, 1991.

Gordon, Mary. *The Shadow Man.* New York: Vintage, 1996.

Greer, Germaine. *Daddy, We Hardly Knew You.* NY: Fawcett, 1989.

Wolff, Geoffrey. *The Duke of Deception: Memories of My Father.* New York: Vintage Books, 1990.

Wolff, Tobias. *This Boy's Life.* Grove Press, 2000.

CONTRIBUTORS

Brooke Anderson

Brooke is currently finishing her memoir of living with chronic illness. She is a native of Los Angeles with a degree in Business Administration and was formerly employed in the field of gerontology. Having raised two children, Brooke has taken her imagination to the written word and has replaced the fantasy of being an actress with the desire to be a world class pool player.

Ruth Bochner (Old War Horse)

History: Concert pianist, Jungian Clay Therapist, Clinical Psychologist. One long marriage; husband handsome and gifted actor. First mate on his sailboats and camp-follower to exotic film locations. Three children, all gems. Presently, memoirist and court advocate for children.

Ruth Bracken

Writing since the age that a pencil fit into her hand, Ruth has written poetry and short stories more for relief and in search of sanity than for the hope of a profession. When she is not scribbling, she designs gardens and is a professional set designer for photographers.

Jacqueline Connolly

A native Californian, she views her life as a trilogy. The first part encompasses her role as mother; the second, her return to college as a mature student; the third, her ventures in the exciting world of self-expression. So far, these endeavors have rewarded Jackie with six children, eight grandchildren, a degree from UCLA, and madcap treks through six continents.

Bairbre Dowling

Conceived at a railway junction in England, born in Dublin, Bairbre grew up in a theatrical family and spent the rest of her life pursuing Acting and Men across Europe and America. Bairbre now lives with her daughter in Los Angeles where she writes, acts, and learns Chinese.

Hillary Horan

Hillary has been writing fiction and memoir for twenty years. She enjoys living in the clean air and cutting-edge environment of Los Angeles' west side with her husband, screenwriter Stu Krieger, and their two children. Hillary has been published in *Redbook*, writing about, what else, her family.

Dorothy S. Huebel

A product of the "Lets Conserve It Generation," whatever *it* is, Dorothy is a recycled administrator-turned-writer, blessed with good health, a sense of humor, and supportive family and colleagues. We can always count on Dorothy for a Monday morning laugh.

Marilyn Kierscey

Marilyn graduated from UCLA and received her MA in Human Development. She works as a researcher for an entertainment company. Her hours at home are spent writing children's stories and memoir pieces, rescuing homeless cats and growing flowers. She is married and has one grown son.

Janet Smith

Never in her wildest imagination as a skinny, scaredy-cat, nose-in-a-book, tow-head growing up during the Depression and World War II in suburban Chicago, would Janet have dreamed her writing would be published in a book. She indulges her memories and love of stories while surrounded by a bouquet of blossoming authors who stimulate her with astonishing revelations of ordinary lives.

EDITOR

Maureen Murdock

Maureen is a native New Yorker living in Santa Barbara, teaching memoir and practicing yoga. For 12 years, Maureen has taught in the UCLA Extension Writers' Program where she met the writers in this anthology. Presently, Maureen is Core Faculty in depth psychology at Pacifica Graduate Institute in Santa Barbara. She is the author of *To the Best of My Recollection*; *The Heroine's Journey*; *Fathers' Daughters*; *Spinning Inward: Using Guided Imagery with Children* and *The Heroine's Journey Workbook*.